# ACADIAN FRENCH
# IN TIME AND SPACE

## A Study in Morphosyntax
## and Comparative Sociolinguistics

# ACADIAN FRENCH
## IN TIME AND SPACE

### A Study in Morphosyntax
### and Comparative Sociolinguistics

RUTH KING

Publication of the American Dialect Society 97

Supplement to *American Speech*, Volume 87

PUBLICATION OF THE AMERICAN DIALECT SOCIETY

*Editor*: ROBERT BAYLEY, *University of California, Davis*
*Managing Editor*: CHARLES E. CARSON, *Duke University Press*

Number 97
Copyright 2013
American Dialect Society
ISBN: 978-0-8223-6784-0

Library of Congress Cataloging-in-Publication Data

King, Ruth Elizabeth, 1954–
    Acadian French in time and space : a study in morphosyntax and comparative
    sociolinguistics / Ruth King.
        pages cm. – (Publication of the American Dialect Society ; number 97)
    Includes bibliographical references and index.
    ISBN 978-0-8223-6784-0 (cloth : alk. paper)
        1. French language–Dialects–Atlantic Provinces. 2. French language–Atlantic
    Provinces. 3. Acadians. I. Title. II. Series: Publication of the American Dialect
    Society ; no. 97.
PC3645.A85K56 2013
447'.97–dc23                                                        2013008515

British Library Cataloguing-in-Publication Data available

*Dedicated to the memory of*

*Lucy Carter King (1914–1972)*

*and*

*Marie Benoît Félix (1923–2011)*

# CONTENTS

# PREFACE

This book synthesizes research on a set of closely related minority language varieties that fall under the general rubric of Acadian French. In addition to my own research on these varieties spanning more than three decades, I draw on the published research of scholars based in North America and in Europe, research that has often appeared only in French. I therefore offer as complete and up-to-date a description of Acadian French as possible, one that is accessible to anglophone audiences.

I begin by setting the stage in terms of the history of the varieties in question (chapter 1) and the methodologies and theories adopted in the present work (chapter 2). Rather than provide a traditional grammatical sketch (see King 2000, chapter 5, in this regard), I have organized the book around a set of topics, including the preservation (or not) of rich verbal morphology and its repercussions (chapter 3), particular points of variation in the system and their exploitation by the grammar (chapter 4), mechanisms involved in the spread of particular instances of grammatical change (chapter 5), and the relationship between discourse phenomena and the grammar (chapter 6). Some linguistic aspects of Acadian French will thus be given extensive treatment while others will be accorded less attention; in the latter case, I will point the reader to the relevant literature.

I have tried to make this book interesting for a number of audiences, including (socio)linguists who focus on the study of grammatical variation and change along with dialectologists interested in the comparison of geographically dispersed but closely-related language varieties. I have also provided information for specialists in other North American varieties, such as Quebec French, along with discussions of particular interest to specialists in socio-syntax and in language contact.

To these ends, this work does not assume much prior familiarity with French in general and any familiarity at all with Acadian French. Examples are given with inter-linear glosses and English translations, and Acadian-specific linguistic features are as far as possible pointed out and referenced. I do not, however, feel the need to put the focus on the set of differences between Acadian French and Standard (or Referential) French, but instead place Acadian French at the center of the discussion. If this book increases the visibility of this language variety and also encourages readers to pursue further some of the ideas or data presented here, it will have fulfilled its goals.

# ACKNOWLEDGMENTS

The idea for this book came to me a long time ago, when I first recognized substantial differences among Acadian French varieties spoken in Newfoundland and Prince Edward Island. The idea to organize the book around particular linguistic themes, rather than simply geographical variation, and to take time depth into account, came much later. First of all, I would like to thank Bob Bayley, PADS series editor, and two anonymous reviewers for constructive comments on the proposal on which the present work is based. Most recently, I thank Bob along with production editor Charles Carson for their work in bringing this project to a smooth and timely conclusion.

Over the years, I have benefited from communication and discussion with a wide variety of scholars. Some are also Acadian or Cadien specialists, including Louise Beaulieu, Wladyslaw Cichocki, Philip Comeau, Carmen LeBlanc, Sylvie Dubois, Karin Flikeid, B. Edward Gesner, Marie-Ève Perrot, Louise Péronnet, and Kevin Rottet. Some are specialists in other North American and European varieties, including Aidan Coveney, Rick Grimm, France Martineau, Raymond Mougeon, Yves Charles Morin, Gillian Sankoff, and Pierrette Thibault. In the early days, the annual meeting of the Atlantic Provinces Linguistic Association was the only place where Acadianists met on a regular basis; I benefited greatly from participating in those meetings. I have since benefited from discussions at the Canadian Linguistic Association, International Conference on Methods in Dialectology, New Ways of Analyzing Variation (NWAV), and Association for French Language Studies conferences. Several other friends and colleagues deserve mention and thanks: Gabriela Alboiu and Yves Roberge for discussion of the theoretical implications of some of my data, and Bob Bayley and James Walker for discussion of quantitative analysis of recalcitrant data. Many anonymous reviewers of my published work have improved the finished products, and comments and questions at numerous conferences have sharpened my thinking about the issues.

Over the years I have engaged in a number of research collaborations: with Gary Butler, Philip Comeau, Sylvie Dubois, France Martineau, Raymond Mougeon, Terry Nadasdi, Yves Roberge, Robert Ryan, and Jeff Tennant. These scholars' own areas of expertise complemented mine, and the final products were much better because of it. Special thanks must go to Gary Butler, whose skills as an ethnographer and narrative specialist allowed me to contextualize my data far better than I could myself. Special thanks must also go to Philip Comeau, whose native-speaker knowledge of Nova Scotian varieties and ability at grammatical analysis enhanced our joint work. Both Gary and Phil read and commented on complete drafts of the present work. All errors are, of course, my own.

My debt to many Acadians is enormous. The people of L'Anse-à-Canards, Newfoundland, along with residents of the nearby communities of Cap St-Georges, La Grand'Terre, and Stephenville/Kippens, welcomed me into their homes and into their lives when I was a young student. Living with the Félix family of L'Anse-à-Canards off and on during the early years taught me the local variety, and it also taught me much about life. I will always value their friendship and that of other community residents. Acadians in small villages in Prince Edward Island and Nova Scotia opened their doors to Gary's and my research assistants, with rates of participation in sociolinguistic interviews probably unheard of in urban contexts. I am also indebted to Alain, Ginette, and Yolande Comeau of Saulnierville Station, Nova Scotia, who have patiently answered my myriad questions about local usage over the past few years. Special thanks go to Prince Edward Island native Robert Gallant for his great help in the construction of the Prince Edward Island sociolinguistic corpus.

The analyses in this book are based on the language use of young and middle-aged Acadians, and of older Acadians, some of whom are no longer with us. I remember in particular Émile Benoît, Joe and Mathilda Bozec, Charles and Marie Cormier, Joséphine Costard, Mary Jo Dubé, Marie Félix, Stanley Formanger, Paul and Maggie Huon, Joe LeRoi, Pierre Secardin, John and Clara White, and Walter and Emily Young. Du fond du coeur, je vous remercie tous.

# ABBREVIATIONS

| | |
|---|---|
| ACC | accusative |
| CA | complicating action narrative clause |
| CO | coda narrative clause |
| DAT | dative |
| EV | evaluation clause |
| F | feminine |
| FUT | future |
| IMP | imperfect |
| IMPER | imperative |
| INF | infinitive |
| M | masculine |
| NEG | negative |
| OR | orientation narrative clause |
| PART | partitive |
| PERS | person |
| PF | periphrastic future |
| PL | plural |
| PP | pluperfect |
| PRES | present |
| PRESP | present perfect |
| Q | interrogative marker |
| REFL | reflexive |
| SG | singular |
| SP | simple past |
| SUBJ | subjunctive |

# 1. THE SOCIOHISTORICAL CONTEXT

THIS BOOK IS CONCERNED with grammatical variation and change in Acadian French, a variety of French spoken in Canada's four Atlantic Provinces (figure 1.1) and in small pockets of the province of Quebec; a close relative, Cajun French, is spoken in Louisiana. In many ways Acadian French is highly conservative, preserving features lost in other French varieties spoken in North America and in Europe, thus providing a sort of window on the past. In other ways, it is innovative, given less contact with normative French than has been the case with many other varieties and given varying degrees of contact with English.

In the present chapter, I set the stage by outlining the history of Acadian settlement in North America, one that involves a number of different settlement waves, changing geopolitical boundaries, and varying degrees of linguistic isolation, both from other varieties of French and from other languages, notably English. These are all key to understanding the social and geographical distribution of present-day varieties as well as similarities and differences that exist among these varieties.

FIGURE 1.1
The Atlantic Provinces of Canada

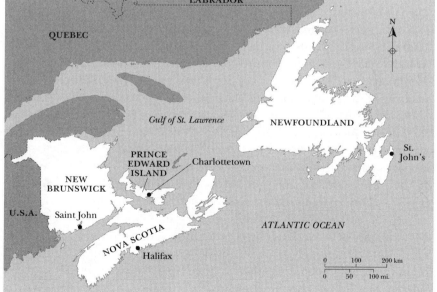

1

## A HISTORICAL OVERVIEW

In 1604, the French explorer Samuel de Champlain and the French no-bleman Pierre du Gua, Sieur de Monts, attempted to settle a small island named Saint Croix in the Bay of Fundy, off the coast of the present-day Canadian province of Nova Scotia. The winter proved hard, and the following spring they moved to the mainland to establish the colony of Port-Royal in that province's Annapolis Valley. Thus, four years before Champlain's founding of New France (i.e., present-day Quebec), a French presence was established on the shores of the Bay of Fundy, the first French-speaking colony in North America. The settlement that grew on these shores differed considerably from New France. Its inhabitants came largely from one particular area of France, the center-west, and were mainly of rural background and members of the lower class (Massignon 1962). On the other hand, New France settlers were of more mixed origins, both geographically (Charbonneau and Guillemette 1994) and socially (Choquette 1997). These sociogeographic differences would have long-lasting effects on dialectal variation.

THE EARLY YEARS OF SETTLEMENT. Settlement at Port-Royal and along the periphery of the Bay of Fundy grew quite independently of New France.[1] France put its resources not into Acadia but into New France since that colony was situated along the banks of the Saint Lawrence River. This location was part of a major transportation route with heavy fortifications along the Saint Lawrence to the north that extended down the Mississippi to the south, thereby containing the English colonies in eastern North America. With the New England colonies as their closest neighbor, French settlers in Acadia would come to have more contact with New England fishermen and merchants than with the francophone residents of New France. The vast majority of these Acadians (the placename *Acadie* was originally applied to peninsular Nova Scotia) came from coastal areas of France, principally from the old provinces of Aunis, Angoumois, Poitou, and Saintonge (see figure 1.2). In France, they had been *saulniers*, builders of dykes and reclaimers of land from the sea, skills that served them well in this part of North America. In the New World, they became subsistence farmers, fishermen, and trappers, or some combination thereof.

By the end of the seventeenth century, the population of Acadia con-sisted mainly of second-to-fourth generation settlers, who formed a social group cohesive enough to allow historians to refer to them from this point on as the Acadian people. Unlike their compatriots to the north, who con-sidered New France the direct extension of France in North America, the

FIGURE 1.2

The Traditional Provinces of France

Acadians considered Acadia, not France, their homeland (see figure 1.3). While the territory nominally changed hands between the French and English a number of times during the seventeenth and early eighteenth centuries, actual ownership had little effect on the lives of the colonists.[2] For instance, American fishermen remained the main trading partners of the Acadians. The Treaty of Utrecht in 1713, which ended the War of the Spanish Succession, gave England ultimate control of Acadia, at a time when the local population numbered between 1,500 and 2,000. While the former French subjects were granted the right to remain neutral in the case of future conflicts between France and England, the exact limits on this neutrality eventually proved to be a contentious issue. By this treaty, France lost Hudson's Bay and peninsular Nova Scotia and maintained only limited fishing rights on the coast of Newfoundland. It did, however, retain Île-Saint-Jean (present-day Prince Edward Island), Île-Royale (now Cape Breton Island, part of the province of Nova Scotia), and the coastline of present-day New Brunswick.[3] The French government invited their former colonists to settle in these areas, and a large number of them did so, leaving British jurisdiction. Despite this exodus, the French population of the

FIGURE 1.3
Acadia in 1749

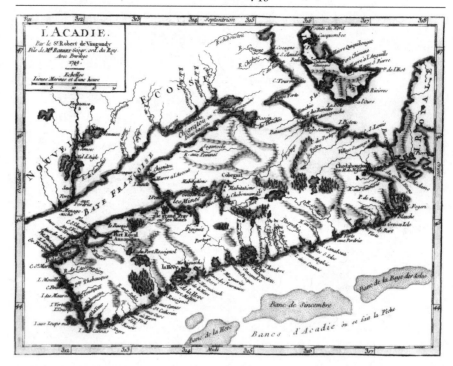

Acadian peninsula would reach approximately 14,000 by the outbreak of the Seven Years' War in 1756.

THE DEPORTATION. The reasons for the *grand dérangement,* or deportation, of 1755 whereby the colonial governor of Nova Scotia, Major Charles Lawrence, ordered the removal of the Acadians from the British colony are controversial. The French had built the fortress of Louisburg on Île-Royale to protect their fleets entering the Gulf of Saint Lawrence. The British reacted by building a fortress at Halifax in 1749. Suspicious of the "French neutrals," as they were called, now present in large numbers and concerned about the strategic location of the Acadian peninsula during wartime, the British deported the Acadians on the grounds that they constituted a security risk. In truth, the latter were actually in possession of highly desirable, arable lands: in fact, the lands vacated by the Acadians were soon occupied by Anglo-American settlers from New England, leading to speculation that threatened security was not the only reason for the deportation. In 1755 alone, some 6,000 people were deported to the New England colonies and

to the West Indies, allowed to take with them only their movable posses-
sions. Indeed, fully 10,000 Acadians would be deported during the period
1755–65, the vast majority of a population estimated to have numbered
about 12,000 in 1750. The deportation continued until 1765, fully two
years after the fall of New France to the British and the end of the Seven
Years' War.

The Protestant New England colonies proved inhospitable to the
Roman Catholic Acadians, and some 3,000 were transported to England
as prisoners of war in 1765, ultimately transferred by treaty arrangement
to France, where they received little support for their plight. This group
would some twenty years later be persuaded to immigrate to Louisiana, con-
stituting a second substantial influx of Acadians to the area (the first group
of approximately 1,000 having arrived there during the deportation itself,
settling in the southwest), while other Acadian exiles in France ended up in
work camps in the French West Indies.

Of those who escaped the deportation, many fled into the wilderness
of what is now New Brunswick and to Prince Edward Island, while others
went to the Gaspé peninsula of present-day Quebec. Still others hid in the
wilderness of Nova Scotia itself. However, following the fall of Louisburg to
the British in 1758, the Acadian settlements on Cape Breton Island and on
Prince Edward Island were also destroyed, with a few families managing to
escape by hiding from the British forces.

THE DEPORTATION'S AFTERMATH. The years following the deportation saw
the dispersal of the Acadian people, to the French islands of Saint-Pierre
and Miquelon off the coast of Newfoundland, to the Îles de la Madeleine
(Magdalen Islands) in the Gulf of Saint Lawrence, and to the highlands of
Cape Breton Island. Returning from exile, beginning in the late 1760s and
lasting a quarter of a century, groups of Acadians settled in Baie Sainte-
Marie and in the Yarmouth-Pubnico regions of what is now Nova Scotia
and at Malpéque, Rustico, and Baie-de-Fortune in Prince Edward Island.
The returning Acadians could not reclaim their original, fertile lands; these
had become the property of the new settlers from New England or, in the
case of Prince Edward Island, of English absentee landlords. The land left
for the Acadians was essentially the land the English themselves did not
want. In the years following their return from exile, Acadians established
isolated settlements where land was available, often surrounded by English
settlements. Relative closeness to English settlements would prove to be
an important predictor of degree and rate of assimilation to English. The
century that followed, leading up to the confederation of Canada (i.e., the
founding of the nation-state) in 1867, would be one of little or no access

to French education and a concomitant lack of an Acadian middle class, in contrast to the conditions of their anglophone neighbors.

The post-deportation Acadian settlements varied in terms of degree of heterogeneity among their settlers. Flikeid (1994) notes that Baie Sainte-Marie and Pubnico saw the return of a significant proportion of former inhabitants of Port-Royal, and these parts of southwestern Nova Scotia have remained the most homogenous of Acadian regions to this day. As we shall see, it is in southwest Nova Scotia that the most conservative variety of Acadian French is spoken. On the other hand, the settlement of Chéticamp, a Nova Scotia community on Cape Breton Island, began relatively late, dating from the early 1780s, and its settlers included Acadians who had been returned to France, others from Prince Edward Island, and still others who had spent time on the islands of Saint-Pierre and Miquelon and the Îles de la Madeleine. As Flikeid observes, the resulting population mixture has made for a certain leveling of distinctively Acadian linguistic features in communities like Chéticamp. Of no particular importance before the deportation, the area that is now northeastern New Brunswick became home to the largest concentration of Acadians, who today comprise more than a third of the population of that province and fully 80% of the population of its northeast section. The settlement of this area also involved the sort of heterogeneity of backgrounds just mentioned for Chéticamp.

The years following the end of the Seven Years' War saw the Acadian people struggle for land. By the Treaty of Paris in 1763, the inhabitants of Lower Canada (i.e., formerly New France, today the province of Quebec) were allowed to retain their lands. Similarly, in 1764 the London Board of Trade established the right of Acadians to settle in the Maritimes if they swore an oath of allegiance to the British sovereign. This right, however, conflicted with a new practice in Prince Edward Island, the granting of land concessions to those British subjects deemed meritorious by the Crown. These latter became (often absentee) landlords, extracting high rents from the Acadians for the right to work the land that the Acadians themselves had cleared. Largely unable to pay these high rents, Acadians searched for available land, some emigrating to Cape Breton Island, some moving to unoccupied concessions. This situation lasted until the time of Canadian confederation in 1867, and resulted in the abandonment of older Prince Edward Island settlements. By the end of the 1830s Acadians in Prince Edward Island were established in the areas of Rollo Bay, Tignish and Cascumpec, Rustico, Miscouche, Baie Egmont, and Mont-Carmel.

The fall of New France had a different effect on the lives of its colonists than did the arrival of British rule on the Acadians. While French government officials in New France returned to France and were replaced by British officials, a form of French civil law was actually retained. Despite wartime setbacks, the French clergy remained, encouraging the survival of the French language, viewed as intimately connected with the survival of the Roman Catholic religion in the New World. Both the clergy and the colonists were convinced that English control was a threat to their language and to their religion, and this led the French population to isolate themselves as much as possible from the British. In contrast to the situation in Acadia, the French population has remained dominant in Quebec (Auger 2005). The link between language and faith was also made by the Acadians and by their clergy, mainly sent out from Quebec. However, the situation was markedly different in Acadia since the local francophone population had no political power and were never served by sufficient numbers of missionaries or priests, particularly by francophone ones. While largely Acadian settlements did exist, many settlements became a mixture of English and French from an early date, leading to the assimilation of their Acadian populations.

## LANGUAGE AND EDUCATION IN NEW BRUNSWICK, PRINCE EDWARD ISLAND, AND NOVA SCOTIA

The early years following the British takeover were ones in which the Acadian people were concerned with the essentials of survival. Many writers of the time remark on the extreme poverty in which many Acadians lived. Even so, as devout Catholics, they regarded the lack of clergy, particularly francophone clergy, as their most pressing concern. Francophone clergy would prove instrumental in the fight for French education, and thus in the fight against assimilation to English culture, whereas anglophone clergy were not necessarily supportive of the cause. In contrast to the situation in Quebec, there were no schools in New Brunswick, Nova Scotia, or Prince Edward Island until the early nineteenth century and most of the population was illiterate. Early Acadian schools, in which the language of instruction was French, were established either by clergy or missionaries, cases in point being those schools founded in Rustico, Prince Edward Island (1815), Caraquet, New Brunswick (1826), and Chéticamp, Nova Scotia (1826).[4] But as the number of schools and the number of pupils increased, lack of qualified teachers became a serious problem; teachers' colleges founded during the nineteenth century in Prince Edward Island and New Brunswick offered instruction only in English, and francophone teachers, if their English was good enough to be admitted, would be instructed in how to teach English. Lack of qualified teachers in Prince Edward Island and Nova

Scotia led to a number of so-called Acadian schools having English as the principal language of instruction. However, the situation in New Brunswick was significantly better since, from the early nineteenth century onward, local parishes had the right to choose their own teachers. Thus, a francophone parish could control the language of instruction. Moreover, in New Brunswick, a tradition of traveling teachers developed, and this provided even small and isolated parishes access to French-language instruction.

The late nineteenth century saw a renaissance of interest in Acadian culture, with concomitant growth in Acadian nationalism in all three Maritime Provinces. This period was marked by the founding of French-language newspapers, such as *Le Moniteur acadien* in New Brunswick (1867), and private colleges, such as the Collège Sainte-Anne in Nova Scotia (1890). Acadian National Conventions (held in Memramcook, N.B., in 1881, Miscouche, P.E.I., in 1884, and Pointe de l'Église, N.S., in 1890) brought together Acadians from all three Maritime Provinces and forged a spirit of nationalism that still resonates. With the Canadian Confederation in 1867, article 133 of the new constitution proclaimed French a national language, not just the language of the new province of Quebec. However, the Acadian cause suffered a serious setback with the passing of school acts that established a uniform school system and a uniform curriculum, with English as the language of instruction regardless of native language or religion. Such laws were passed in Nova Scotia (1864), New Brunswick (1871), and Prince Edward Island (1877). Only in privately funded institutions, for which resources were scarce, could French be the language of instruction.

In Nova Scotia, the law was strictly enforced. It was not until 1905 that a new law permitted the use of French readers in the first five grades; in the higher grades, instruction was exclusively in English. A few convent schools, notably the one at Chéticamp, the seminary in Halifax, and the private College Sainte-Anne at Pointe de l'Église, kept French education alive in Nova Scotia. Not surprisingly, there was much assimilation to English. Today, there are five main francophone areas in Nova Scotia (Pubnico, Pomquet, Île-Madame, Chéticamp, and Baie Sainte-Marie), but only in Chéticamp and Baie Sainte-Marie are there substantial French populations.[5] It was not until 1982 and the passing of the Canadian Charter of Rights and Freedoms that the right of the francophone minority to an education in French was officially recognized in Canada. That date marked the beginning of French-medium schooling in southwest Nova Scotia (along, of course, with the existing Collège Sainte-Anne, now officially a university). In Pomquet and Île-Madame, the system in place until quite recently was a "French immersion" program, designed for nonnative speakers, which disregards the fact that many of the Acadian children are francophones. The establishment of such programs, in which the emphasis is on Standard French (in French, *français de référence*) with little regard for the home language, is certainly better than system with "French as but one school subject," but it cannot help but reinforce the distance that exists between the vernacular and so-called good French.[6] The opening of true French-medium schools in Pomquet and Île-Madame took place only at the debut of the 2000/01 school year.

As in Nova Scotia, the school act led to the creation of a number of private schools in Prince Edward Island. As mentioned above, trained francophone teachers were hard to find as the teachers' college in Charlottetown provided only English instruction. In Rollo Bay, Casumpec, Miscouche, and Tignish, communities with mixed populations, assimilation to English was already pronounced by the 1880s. However, the situation was somewhat better in Prince Edward Island than in Nova Scotia in that Acadians were able to obtain a number of concessions from the provincial government. For instance, in 1891 schools in Acadian school districts were finally able to obtain French textbooks. A bilingual inspector, a native Acadian, was named for these schools. Associations such as the Société Saint-Thomas d'Aquin and the Association des instituteurs et institutrices acadiens de l'Île-du-Prince-Édouard became important advocates for francophone rights in education. In 1936, there were still 45 schools in which Acadian pupils were in the majority and in which French was taught, a striking contrast to the situation in Nova Scotia.

Beginning in the late 1950s, efforts by the Prince Edward Island government to streamline the education system had the effect of strengthening the French language in one part of the island but of hastening its decline in the rest. Large consolidated schools were built, replacing many of the small district schools, including most of the Acadian schools. In the Évangéline region, which includes the communities of Abram-Village, Baie-Egmont, Mont-Carmel, and Wellington, the École Régionale Évangéline was built in 1960. With the government's blessing, the standard English-language curriculum was supplemented with a French program of instruction. French soon became the language of administration and most school activities. For the other Acadian communities on the island, district schools were replaced by the English-language consolidated schools, with the result that Acadian children in Tignish, Palmer Road, Saint-Louis, Bloomfield, Miscouche, Rustico North and South, and Hope River were exposed to French only in French-as-a-second-language classes, programs beginning as early as the third grade or as late as the seventh grade. Although these communities were not as overwhelmingly French as those of the Évangéline region, they did have many residents for whom French was the first language. The 1960s, then, saw heightened sensitivity on the part of the provincial government toward the French language, but only for the Évangéline region, where the École Évangéline has supplied French-medium education since the late 1970s and where French remains the dominant language of the area.[7] In the Tignish region, the school system remained English, with the development of a French immersion stream since the 1970s. My 1987 Prince Edward Island French sociolinguistic corpus provides evidence that young graduates of the Tignish school display a markedly different command of French from their counterparts in Évangéline who had attended the French-medium school (and, of course, live in a French-majority region). It would take more than a decade before a French-medium school in the Tignish area, École Pierre-Chiaisson located in the village of Deblois, would open its doors in 2001.

In New Brunswick, a relatively high fertility rate from the late nineteenth through to the mid-twentieth century actually increased the proportion of the francophone population from 16% of the population in 1871 to 46% of the population in 1992 (Allard and Landry 1998, 205). During the years following the passing of the school act of 1871, clergy and traveling teachers were successful in supplementing the English-language school system. The early twentieth century saw the beginning of summer courses for French teachers and the establishment of important support groups for these teachers. New Brunswick has thus not experienced as serious a shortage of francophone teachers or francophone clergy as have the two other Maritime Provinces. The relative size of this population has been key to the establishment of French-language institutions. Founded in 1963, the Université de Moncton is the largest French-language university in Canada outside of Quebec. The Official Languages Act of 1969 made New Brunswick Canada's only officially bilingual province. In 1981, the (provincial) Act Representing the Equality of the Two Official Languages was passed in New Brunswick, and in that same year anglophone and francophone communities were granted control over their own systems of school administration, abolishing bilingual schools in francophone communities in favor of French-medium schools.


## THE ACADIAN PRESENCE IN NEWFOUNDLAND

As noted above, Acadian French is spoken in Newfoundland as well as in the Maritime Provinces (New Brunswick, Nova Scotia, and Prince Edward Island), a fact not mentioned in many of the histories of Acadia or in many linguistic works on Acadian French prior to the last decade.[8] The settle-

ment of the Port-au-Port Peninsula of western Newfoundland by Acadians
is often lost amid the many migrations of small groups of Acadians following the deportation. However, maritime records show Acadian families
settling in the Baie Saint-Georges/Port-au-Port Peninsula area of the province's west coast from the 1770s on. That their history is not well known is
perhaps explained by the fact that, following the Treaty of Utrecht and the
granting of fishing rights to the French along the so-called French shore
of Newfoundland, all settlement between Cape Bonavista to the north and
along the west coast to Point Riche to the south was in theory forbidden.
However, despite the treaty's conditions, by the mid-1850s there were approximately 1,500 settlers in the area, including English and Scottish settlers and Mi'kmaq from Cape Breton Island, along with the Acadians, who
formed the majority of the small population. Some of the Acadians came
directly from Cape Breton Island; others arrived by way of the Îles de la
Madeleine and the French islands of Saint-Pierre and Miquelon, where
they had sought refuge following the deportation.

The history of Newfoundland's Acadian population differs markedly
from that of the Maritime Provinces in that they were joined in Newfoundland, from the 1830s on, by substantial numbers of French from France.
Some of this latter group were adult males who deserted from the French
navy and were engaged in fishing off the coast; others were whole families
from Saint-Pierre and Miquelon who were stationed by the French on the
Newfoundland coast to protect their fishing facilities. With the termina-
tion of the French fishery on the Treaty Shore in 1904 and the subsequent
departure of the French fleets, many of these families chose to stay in Newfoundland, their home for many years. The French vessels fishing off the
Newfoundland coast worked out of ports in northwestern France, mainly in
Normandy and Brittany. Thus, the European settlers would have differed
from the Acadians in place of origin in France and in the variety of French
spoken. Interestingly, a number of the new "French" settlers actually spoke
Breton as a first language, but almost all traces of it have since died out.[9]

The French-speaking settlers of the Saint-Georges area of western Newfoundland, which included the communities of Saint-Georges, Stephenville, and Kippens, were predominantly Acadian, whereas the nearby Port-
au-Port Peninsula had more mixed European/Acadian settlement, with
communities established at Île-Rouge (later settlement moved from this
small island to La Grand'Terre, on the mainland), Cap Saint-Georges, and
Maisons d'Hiver/L'Anse-à-Canards. At the turn of the century, the peninsula had approximately 1,500 inhabitants, and Stephenville and Kippens
together had about 1,000, with anglophones a distinct minority in both
areas. Assimilation to English took place early at Saint-Georges as a result of

substantial Scottish settlement during the latter half of the nineteenth century. Given the fact that permanent settlement was still at least nominally forbidden, the area remained quite isolated, with transportation mainly by boat and no schools or churches established until late in the nineteenth century.

English influence was first most strongly felt in the school system. The schools that were established on Newfoundland's west coast were run by unilingual English teachers and the language of instruction was always English. Not surprisingly, few francophone children remained in school long. In addition, an event that had a major impact on the population of this isolated area was to take place at the beginning of World War II: the United States Air Force established an airbase at Harmon Field on the outskirts of Stephenville, buying for nominal sums rich agricultural land farmed by the Acadians. The population of Stephenville greatly increased during the war as people from all parts of Newfoundland moved there in search of work at the airbase and in related industries. Many of the local French worked there as well, learning English in order to get jobs. The introduction of radio and, later, television was also an important factor in assimilation to English, since until the 1970s only English-language programming was provided. Today in Stephenville and Kippens, French has almost entirely died out: in the course of fieldwork I conducted in 1980, fewer than half a dozen fluent French speakers could be found, whereas 40 years earlier the majority of the population of approximately 1,000 had been French-speaking.

On the more isolated Port-au-Port Peninsula, however, where fishing had remained the principal means of employment, assimilation to English proceeded at a much slower rate. In 1937, an English community was established at Clam Bank Cove, some five miles from L'Anse-é-Canards and 20 miles from La Grand'Terre. However, up until the mid-1980s, the francophone communities could only be reached by gravel road and the majority of the adult residents remained French speaking. Nevertheless, years of contact with English and second-class status for French had taken their toll. In the 1950s and 60s, many French Newfoundlanders encouraged their children to learn English and stopped speaking French in the home, feeling that French would only be a burden to them. English was viewed as the language of better paying jobs and community services, and French survived only as a home language. It was not until the 1980s that French immersion, followed by true French-medium education, would become available to residents of Newfoundland's francophone west coast.

## THE PRESENT-DAY SITUATION

Table 1.1 gives an overview of French language presence in the four Atlantic Provinces as measured by French (versus English or other) mother tongue in the 2006 Canadian census. In Newfoundland and Labrador, Nova Scotia, and Prince Edward Island, French is spoken by a small proportion of the population, with concentrations of Acadian speakers in fairly isolated regions. In contrast, in New Brunswick, French is spoken by a third of the population, a proportion that has remained stable for decades. It has had the status of an official language at the provincial (as well as national) level since 1969, as noted above. There are three main dialect areas in New Brunswick: (1) the northwest (known as *le Madawaska*, which comprises Madawaska county and parts of Restigouche and Victoria counties) and includes large towns such as Edmunston; (2) the northeast, which comprises Gloucester county and parts of Northumberland and Restigouche and is usually referred to as *la péninsule acadienne* ('the Acadian peninsula'), which includes villages popular with tourists, such as Caraquet; and (3) the southeast, which comprises Moncton and the surrounding area, along with the towns of Newcastle and Chatham (see figure 1.4). In Madawaska and particularly on the Acadian peninsula, French is a majority language: indeed in the latter case well over 90% of residents have French as their mother tongue (Beaulieu 1996). The Madawaska variety, called *brayon*, displays a number of features that may be accounted for in terms of the Quebec origins of a portion of its settlers or in terms of the present-day dialect contact situation that exists on the Quebec–New Brunswick border (McKillop 1987). As for the Acadian peninsula, it is considered to have been least influenced by English due to its relative isolation and high concentration of francophones. As Flikeid (1989b, 185) notes, "The internal cohesion of the community and the high rates of French language use in most areas

### TABLE 1.1
2006 Census Results for Mother Tongue for the Four Atlantic Provinces
(Statistics Canada 2006)

|  | *New Brunswick* | *Nova Scotia* | *Prince Edward Island* | *Newfoundland and Labrador* |
|---|---|---|---|---|
| Total population | 719,650 | 903,090 | 134,205 | 500,610 |
| English mother tongue | 463,190 | 832.105 | 125,260 | 488,405 |
| French mother tongue | 232,975 | 32,540 | 5,345 | 1,885 |
| English and French | 4,450 | 2,100 | 495 | 295 |
| Other | 19,035 | 5905 | 3105 | 10,025 |

FIGURE 1.4
Present-Day New Brunswick

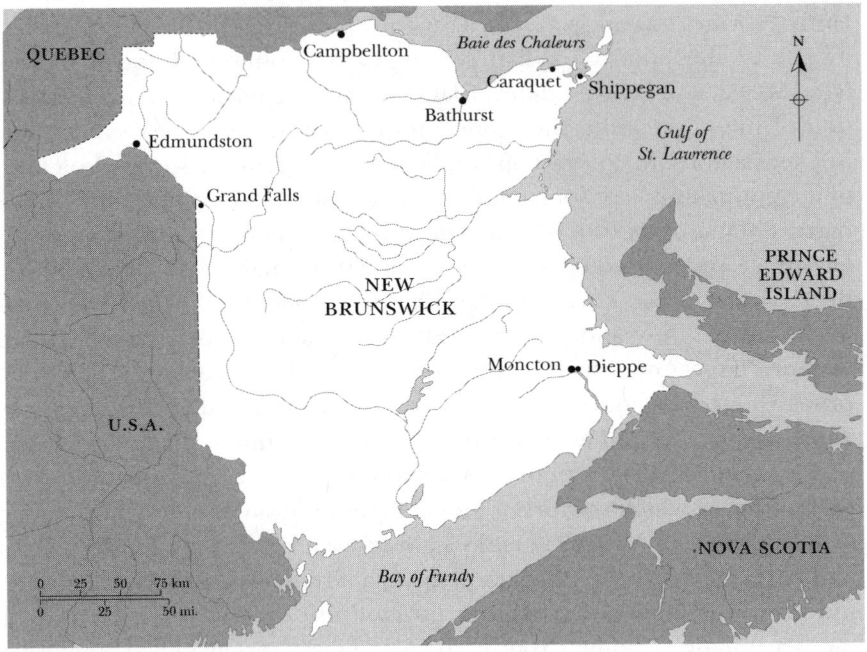

of communication are exceptional among francophone areas outside of Quebec" (my translation).[10]

It is in the southeast of the province that French is in a minority position: only a third of southeastern New Brunswick's 115,815 residents were francophone at the time of the 2006 census, a long-standing situation since the same proportion was found in 1976, the time of the first major study of the French of Moncton, the province's second largest city (Roy 1979).[11]

The proportion of French speakers in Nova Scotia is comparable to that found in Prince Edward Island, with around 4% of the population reporting French as their mother tongue. There are five main Acadian areas of the province (see figure 1.5). As was seen earlier, Chéticamp and Baie Sainte-Marie have the largest French populations and the most services available in French while Pubnico, Pomquet, and Île-Madame are more assimilated. Pubnico relies on the English community of Yarmouth for many essential services, while Pomquet is close to the English town of Antigonish. Pomquet and Île-Madame have obtained French medium schooling only recently and then through the provision of French immersion classes, as noted above. Flikeid (1989a) conducted a self-report survey and compiled statistics regarding the use of French versus English in the

FIGURE 1.5
Present-Day Nova Scotia

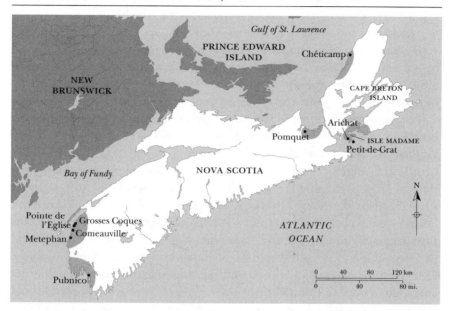

daily lives of residents of the five areas and found the following rank ordering, beginning with most French use: Chéticamp, Baie Sainte-Marie, Pubnico, Île-Madame, and Pomquet.

While the situation of Acadians in Prince Edward Island in some ways compares favorably to that of their Nova Scotia counterparts, there has in fact been a gradual decline in the number of francophones in Prince Edward Island since 1931. Of the 3,420 Islanders who spoke French in the home at the time of the the 1981 federal census, the first Canadian census in which the question was asked, over 96% lived in Prince County, which includes both the Tignish and the Évangéline regions; the 1991 figures show a similar concentration, with 86% (2,930 people) of the total population speaking French as the home language living in Prince County. In the Tignish region, which includes the towns of Palmer Road, Saint-Louis, and the town of Tignish, we find that 2,306 people, 45% of the population were of French origin in 1981, but only 25.6% claimed to speak French as a first language and a mere 17.7% reported speaking French at home.[12] By 1991 the numbers were 1,654 people of French origin, just over 36% of respondents, with 26.9% of the total population giving French as their first language and only 11% as the home language. In 1981, 66% of those who reported speaking French as their mother tongue continued to speak French as a home language; by 1991 the figure had fallen to 40%. In the

Évangéline region, the 1981 census found 2,900 people, 47% of the population, to be of French origin with 37% of the total population speaking French as a first language and 32% speaking it in the home.

Crucially, certain communities—Abram-Village, Wellington, and environs—had large percentages of the population reporting to be of French origin, with French as their mother tongue AND home language (see figure 1.6). In Abram-Village, site of the École Évangéline, 325 of 351 residents were of French origin in 1981, with 275 speaking French as a first language and 255 speaking French in the home. An additional 30 respondents gave both French and English as their mother tongues, and 15 gave French and English as their home languages. According to the 1991 census, 2,000 people in Évangéline stated they were of French origin, 58% of the population, while 56% claimed French as their mother tongue and 50% reported speaking it in the home. In 1991, the population of Abram-Village had fallen to 311 with 260 of (uniquely) French origin, 275 with French as their first language, and 270 as the home language.[13] The most striking comparison between Évangéline and Tignish regions is found when we contrast French ethnic origin and French mother tongue figures with French home language figures. In Évangéline in 1981, 70% of those who claimed French ethnic origin reported speaking French as their home language, and 85% of those who claimed French as their mother tongue reported speaking

FIGURE 1.6
Present-Day Prince Edward Island

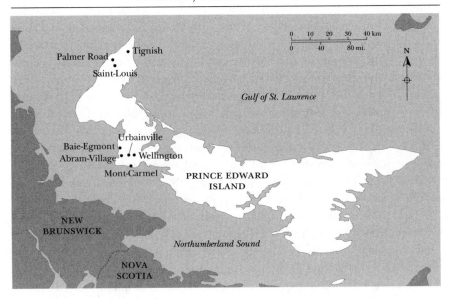

French as their home language; in 1991 the figures were 85% and 89%, respectively. In Tignish in 1981, 39% of those who claimed French ethnic origin reported speaking French as their home language, and 66% of those who claimed French as their mother tongue reported speaking French as their home language; in 1991 the figures were 22% and 40%, respectively.

In his 1987 book *Les Acadiens de l'Île*, Georges Arsenault cites a number of reasons for the decline of French in Prince Edward Island, including the lack of education in French for Acadians outside of Évangéline, the absence of francophone clergy in some parishes, the influence of English television, and the need for young Acadians to move to English-speaking urban areas, such as Summerside and Charlottetown, in search of work, with urbanization often leading to exogamous marriages (and failure to transmit French to offspring). In Évangéline, French remains the language of the school, the church, and community affairs. In the other regions of the province, French is at best a home language with little status.

In the 1970s, the national emphasis on bilingualism and biculturalism led to a reemergence of interest in French in western Newfoundland. The provincial government still ignored the French presence on the island, but in 1971, Port-au-Port Peninsula/Bay Saint-George was declared a bilingual federal district by the federal government (see figure 1.7). Since that time, federal grants from the office of the Secretary of State have supported com-

**FIGURE 1.7**
Francophone Area of Present-Day Newfoundland

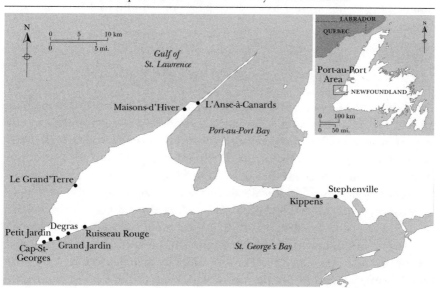

munity projects aimed at the preservation of French, such as the coordination of local francophone associations, and French Newfoundlanders are now represented in the Société Nationale des Acadiens. Some efforts have been successful in the area of French schooling, with French immersion in place in Cap Saint-Georges since the 1970s and French-language primary education in La Grand'Terre since 1989. However, despite the fact that some writers claim the number of those who speak French as a home language is as high as 3,000, I estimated the actual number of fluent French speakers to be somewhere between 400 and 1,000 at the time of fieldwork conducted in 1980.[14] The assimilation years since World War II have resulted in many French Newfoundlanders under the age of 40 who do not speak French. Thus, while the past 20 years have brought enormous changes to the Port-au-Port Peninsula, including renewed pride in French heritage, efforts may have been too late to preserve French as a first language.

Economic issues have also had an impact on the small communities where French is still spoken. For instance, since the collapse of the traditional fishing industry in the early 1990s, Newfoundland's francophones have been part of a rural exodus, which has seen Cap Saint-Georges, for example, lose 15% of its population between 1996 and 2001. Further, Magord, Landry, and Allard's (2002) study shows that a decline in ethnolinguistic vitality took place in the 1990s, such that students interviewed in 1998 were much less likely to use French in different domains of interaction than were their 1991 counterparts and were less integrated into the local francophone community. In a 2005 overview article, King and Butler lament what would appear to be the passing of a traditional language and culture.

## THE ACADIAN DIASPORA

Today, then, the descendants of the original Acadian settlers live in the four Atlantic Provinces but form a substantial proportion of the population only in New Brunswick. The reasons for the decline of French in the three other provinces are quite similar. In the Maritime Provinces and in Newfoundland, the French language has best survived in areas where the Acadians have been isolated geographically from the English majority.

It should be noted that Acadian French is also spoken outside of the Atlantic Provinces. Pockets of Acadian settlement, dating from the years just before and following the deportation, can be found in southern Quebec, in communities called Les Petites Cadies by their settlers, on Quebec's Gaspé Peninsula and in the Îles de la Madeleine in the Gulf of Saint Lawrence, and in Miquelon, one of the two French islands off the south coast of Newfoundland. The Îles de la Madeleine variety is interesting for a number of reasons. Francophones form a very strong majority and have been isolated for centuries from other French varieties, an isolation only overcome in the late twentieth century. Thus, this variety would provide a baseline for Acadian French spoken with little contact with English and with supralocal varieties of French. Further, while settlers from Cape Breton Island formed the majority of francophone settlers to western Newfoundland, there were also a substantial number of settlers from the Îles de la Madeleine, part of the dispersal and regroupment of the Acadian people in the years following the deportation.[15]

It is also the case that French-Canadian settlement (i.e., secondary settlement by residents of Quebec) has exerted some influence on the French spoken in the Atlantic Provinces. In New Brunswick, in the upper Saint John River Valley is the area known as Madawaska. Dialect mixture has also taken place here, since in the late eighteenth century the area was settled by both Acadians and French Canadians from the area of the present-day county of Kamouraska in Quebec. The area of this mixed settlement includes what is now the extreme north of the state of Maine, a territory ceded by Britain to the United States in 1842. Thus, one speaks of the Madawaska region in terms of *le Madawaska canadien* and *le Madawaska américain*. Small pockets of mixed Acadian-Quebec settlement are still to be found in New Hampshire and Connecticut (Fox and Smith 2005).

Finally, a discussion of the history of the Acadian people would not be complete without mentioning perhaps the best known group of descendants of the original Acadian settlers, the Cajuns of Louisiana, descendants of the exiled Acadians of the mid-eighteenth century, who arrived in Louisiana over a 20-year period from the mid- to late 1700s. A first wave of Acadians, numbering about 1,000, settled in the southwest between 1755 and 1769, in prairie parishes such as Saint Landry and Vermilion (see figure 1.8). Other francophones, French colonists from France, had begun arriving in the area in 1698, settling in New Orleans and along the Mississippi River. A second wave of Acadians, just under 900, who had originally been exiled to France, arrived in 1785 and settled in present-day Lafourche and Terrebonne Parishes. A third francophone group, slaves from the island of Saint-Domingue (now Haiti), arrived in the early 1800s, entering the local plantation system. Like the first wave of Acadians, they lived primarily in the southwestern part of the state (Brasseaux 1998). Planter/slave contact resulted in the development of Lousiana French Creole. From the late 1600s until the Lousiana Purchase of 1803, whereby the colony was ceded to the United States, French was the dominant language in Louisiana.

FIGURE 1.8
French Parishes of Louisiana

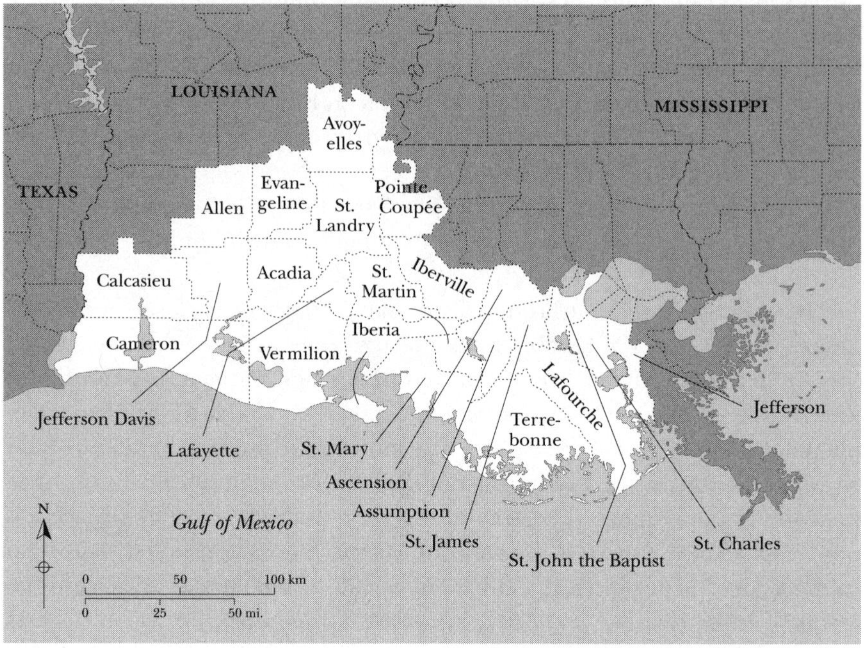

Despite statehood in 1812, French remained strong due to the elevated status of the descendants of the European French settlers. Serious erosion of French dates only from the 1920s, when English was recognized as the official language of the state, thereby reducing greatly the use of French in New Orleans and making English the predominant language of education and religion. Contact with English grew in southwestern Louisiana with the building of major roadways, with the draft in World War II, and with work opportunities attracting francophones to Texas in the postwar oil boom. These developments resulted in a generation of young people who did not transmit French to their children. During this postwar period, use of French became highly stigmatized.

In the 1980s and 1990s, estimates of the number of actual French speakers varied greatly, a range caused by people's extreme reluctance, at least until the late twentieth century, to admit to being French-speaking. Rottet (2001, 68) notes that the number of people in Louisiana who claimed to speak French as a home language in the 1990 U.S. Census was 261,678, some 6.8% fewer than in 1980, while linguists' accounts have suggested the numbers to be higher. In recent years, there has been a revival of interest in Cajun culture, both locally and nationally. A number of writers suggest that efforts being made to promote the language and culture may ultimately have a positive effect on the process of language shift (Brown 1993). However, Dubois and Horvath (1999) suggest that it is Cajun English, rather than Cajun French, that has become the linguistic locus of Cajun identity: for young (male) Cajuns, French-accented English functions as symbolic capital in what has come to be known as the Cajun Renaissance. In this book, I will try as far as is possible to make links between spoken Acadian and Cajun French, although the task is a difficult one, given the heterogeneity of Louisiana French settlement and the lengthy time period separating Cajun French from its Atlantic Canada origins.

## CONCLUSION

While many tend to view speakers of Canadian French as a homogenous group, we see that the two main groups of French settlers of present-day Canada, those of New France and Acadia, have lived largely in isolation from each other and have undergone very different evolutions. Further, the Acadian communities of Atlantic Canada differ in terms of degree of homogeneity of settlement (compare in this regard Baie Sainte-Marie, Nova Scotia, and the Prince Edward Island Acadian communities), amount of contact with English (for example, the Newfoundland communities versus Île-Madame and Pubnico in Nova Scotia), and contact with external varieties of French (for example, Chéticamp, Nova Scotia, versus Tignish, Prince Edward Island).

# 2. DATA, METHOD, AND THEORY

THIS CHAPTER OUTLINES a methodological and theoretical perspective on language variation and change that I have developed over the years, a perspective that combines insights from variationist linguistics, formal grammatical theory, and ethnographically oriented discourse analysis, approaches not typically brought together. However, it turns out that this integration works quite well in the investigation of grammatical variation along with the implementation and spread of change and its representation in the grammar(s) involved.

This chapter also lays out the sources of the data on which the present work is based, which include data from large sociolinguistic interview corpora, folklore recordings of artistic performances, written records on the history of the language, such as late-nineteenth-century informal letters and satirical texts, and secondary sources, such as theses, dissertations, and dialect atlases, along with the usual scholarly forms of publication. I also occasionally provide supplementary linguistic evidence derived from data elicitation with native-speaker consultants. Here as elsewhere in this book, I make no assumptions about the reader's knowledge of French but lay out data as "foreign-language" material.

## VARIATION AND THE HISTORICAL RECORD

In some respects the historical record for Acadian French is quite rich. The data available to the contemporary researcher include important works: a major, primarily lexical study based on fieldwork dating from the 1940s (Massignon 1962); a dialect atlas for the three Maritime Provinces (Péronnet et al. 1998); dialectal descriptions dating from the late nineteenth century (e.g., Poirier 1884; Geddes 1893–94, 1908); and linguistic analyses based on large sociolinguistic corpora from the 1970s–1990s for the French spoken in all four Atlantic Provinces and French Louisiana (e.g., Flikeid 1989a, 1989b; King 1991; Beaulieu 1994; Butler 1995; Dubois 1995; Rottet 2001). While the written record is actually slighter than is the case for Laurentian French,[1] understandable given the history outlined in chapter 1, early documentation exists in the form of nineteenth-century satirical texts published in Acadian newspapers (e.g., Gérin and Gérin 1982) and informal letters from the late nineteenth century (e.g., Martineau and Tailleur 2011). And while it can be argued that an Acadian literary tradition only emerged in the second half of the twentieth century, there exists a wealth of folklore recordings of oral literature dating from the late 1940s and 1950s.[2]

Given the diversity of these data sources, there is a risk, well known to historical linguists, in making direct comparisons of the data contained therein. As the Acadian linguist Louise Péronnet (1995, 39) notes, traditional folktales such as those recorded in Acadian communities in the 1950s and 1960s give us access to the history of a language but serve as no more than an indirect point of comparison with everyday speech:

In its position as a document transmitted orally (lit. from mouth to ear) from one generation to the next, the folktale reproduces above all the language of the past.... It reflects oral language in its most literary usage. [my translation][3]

Thus, in this book data from what Bauman (1977) has termed artistic performance and Coupland (2007) high performance will be used judiciously, and wherever possible they will be one of a number of data sources for a given locale or period. Where I am obliged to rely uniquely on data from oral literature or from written representations, I will be clear about the status of the representation and the kind of inferences we may draw. As we shall see, for the earli(er) stages in the history of vernacular usage, our analyses are on safest ground when the data from a number of different data sources coincide (see King, Martineau, and Mougeon 2011 for discussion).

Let's take as an example a linguistic feature that has to be regarded as a conservative feature of the spoken language, use of the simple past (in French, the *passé simple*), or preterite. This tense has actually been supplanted in most spoken French varieties by the compound form, the present perfect (the *passé composé*), since the turn of the nineteenth century. In 1946, the French linguist and folklorist Geneviève Massignon recorded a Baie Sainte-Marie, Nova Scotia, octogenarian telling the traditional folktale *The Children and the Ogre* (AT 327).[4] We will consider this short text in more detail in the next chapter, but note here that the first 25 complicating action clauses—that is, clauses that provide an answer to the question "And what happened next?" (Labov and Waletzky 1967)—involve use of the simple past, while the following nine involve the present perfect. The variation found in the text can be related to temporal distance from the moment of speech, a well-known constraint on the expression of past temporal reference in French: more distant events are rendered in the simple past, while more recent ones are rendered in the present perfect. Thus, the text itself shows robust use of a linguistic feature usually considered to be at best moribund in spoken French. What we cannot tell, however, is the status of the simple past in the everyday speech of this particular consultant or his peers. The text appears as an appendix to Massignon's (1947) short article describing features of Acadian French, in which she observes that use of the simple past is very much alive in Acadia.

While Massignon did do fieldwork in the three Maritime Provinces and in Acadian-speaking parts of Quebec, we should not necessarily assume that use of the simple past was widespread throughout. For instance, no mention is made of such usage in the American linguist James Geddes's 1908 Ph.D. dissertation on the Acadian variety of Baie de Chaleurs, New Brunswick, right on the Quebec–New Brunswick border.[5] However, Gesner's (1979a) description of the Baie Sainte-Marie, Nova Scotia, variety (i.e. the area where Massignon had recorded the 1947 version of the folktale) is based on the speech of 8 individuals (4 of whom were middle-aged and 4 elderly) recorded in 1976 and 1977. His study includes discussion of the occurrence of 42 tokens of the simple past (versus 306 tokens of the present perfect) in his corpus. The four extracts that Gesner provides all come from narratives of personal experience (Gesner 1979a, 36). Comeau, King, and Butler (2012) coded Gesner's data for (Labovian) clause type and found that the great majority of complicating action clauses involved use of the simple past.

Flikeid and Péronnet's (1989) study of the usage of traditional Acadian variants for a number of variables by older speakers of New Brunswick and Nova Scotia varieties is very important for our purposes.These authors make cross-dialectal comparisons for a number of linguistic features: for instance, they find that *point*, rather than *pas*, is the general negator in Baie Sainte-Marie and nearby Pubnico, pointing to the conservative nature of southwest Nova Scotia varieties.[6] However, with regard to verbal morphology, Flikeid and Péronnet do not actually quantify use of the homophonous simple past or imperfect subjunctive (the *imparfait du subjonctif*) because of the perceived difficulty (and, perhaps as well, the time-consuming process) of distinguishing the two. They do note, though, that while use of the imperfect subjunctive was found in both provinces, use of the simple past seemed to be limited to the Acadian regions of Nova Scotia, including Baie Sainte-Marie, in their corpora.

In Comeau, King, and Butler (2012), we undertook the first large-scale quantitative analysis of past temporal reference in Acadian French, based on data from a 1990–91 sociolinguistic corpus for the Baie Sainte-Marie community of Grosses Coques. These data, recorded almost 50 years after Massignon's fieldwork, reveal substantial usage of the simple past and, most importantly, show usage conditioned by temporal distance from the moment of speech, as it is described in grammatical commentary on the history of the language (Fournier 1998). Thus, it is not surprising that we get a hint of this constraint in the Massignon text. At the end of the exercise, then, we can conclude that with regard to the expression of past temporal reference, Massignon aptly described usage in the Baie Sainte-Marie of the 1940s, but probably not in all of the Acadian areas of Atlantic Canada, a point to which we return in chapter 3.

The time depth we have for Baie Sainte-Marie, Nova Scotia, is not, however, matched for a number of the other Acadian varieties, such as Newfoundland Acadian French. First, there are no written or oral records for this variety prior to the 1950s, and even then they are limited to a particular artistic genre, the traditional folksong. The earliest audio recordings come from the ethnomusicologist Kenneth Peacock's *Songs of the Newfoundland Outports* (1965), for which Peacock recorded the singer Joséphine LeCostard (1904–82) of the village of Cap Saint-Georges from 1959 to 1961.[7] The ethnographer Gary Butler (1995) also provides a (contextualized) selection of Madame LeCostard's songs, learned from her (Metropolitan) French father and grandfather, several of which contain examples of the simple past. Butler and I both recorded Madame LeCostard several times in the late 1970s and early 1980s, in both high performance and in conversation. Butler (1995, 174–80) gives the complete text of her version of *La main coupée*, AT 706 *The Maiden without Hands*, a folktale that she learned from her grandfather, a Français de France ('Frenchmen from France') named Léon Dubé. This text includes 79 instances of the historic present (the *présent historique*) and 13 instances of the present perfect (note that frequent verb forms like *dit* 'say' may be an instance of either the historic present or the simple past and are not included in this count). Unambiguous simple past usage is entirely absent from Madame LeCostard's performance of the folktale, as it is from all our recordings for this consultant outside of folksong performance.

Since the 1970s, there has been an enormous surge of research on Newfoundland French varieties, such that we now have at our disposal large interview corpora for all four communities in which French was or is still spoken. Some of this research (e.g., Thomas 1983; Butler 1990) has been concerned with the local storytelling tradition: however, in Newfoundland (unlike in Baie Sainte-Marie, Nova Scotia), the historic present (in variation with the present perfect) is THE narrative tense in both the performance of traditional folktales and in the performance of narratives of personal experience. Further, our large sociolinguistic corpora for French Newfoundland contain no unambiguous uses of the simple past outside of traditional folksong.[8] Thus, while the past temporal reference data from Massignon's Baie Sainte-Marie, Nova Scotia, traditional folktale are indeed in line with "everyday" usage, this is not the case for French Newfoundland, where we see that the simple past is limited to one particular artistic genre. Recall that the French Newfoundland case is one of nineteenth-century dialect contact: it may well be that in this context leveling of particular grammatical features ensued.[9]

These comparisons, then, show the utility of considering a range of data sources and of examining all of the extant data for a particular linguistic feature or geographical area. The choice of variable discussed here was not arbitrary, in that we would expect the simple past to turn up in narration in the artistic genres, all other things being equal. Generally, attending to discourse mode (e.g., narrative versus conversation) has proven important in our understanding of a number of variable usages in Acadian French. For instance, King, Nadasdi, and Butler (2004) found that while the traditional first-person plural variant *je . . . ons* (e.g., *je parlons* 'we are speaking') is receding in the speech of Abram-Village, Prince Edward Island, due to influence from supralocal varieties, the variant has not simply faded away but has come to serve particular discourse functions in the performance of personal experience and community narratives.

Another data source which must be treated with care are satirical texts, such as a set of famous letters, 16 in total, said to have been written by a (stereotypical) late-nineteenth-century Acadian housewife, Marichette. The letters were published in the Acadian newspaper *L'Évangéline* between 1895 and 1898. Gérin and Gérin's 1982 annotated edition, *Marichette: Lettres acadiennes*, provides excellent contextualization of these letters, the community in which "Marichette" lived, and the particular period in Acadian society. Like other highly self-conscious expressions of language and identity, though, the relationship of the language of the letters to the vernacular of the period is complex. For instance, the writer chooses particular linguistic features to index Acadianess: third-person plural *ils . . . ont* (e.g., *ils parlont* 'they are speaking' vs. Standard French *ils parlent*, the latter with a phonetically null inflectional ending) is near categorical, and *je . . . ons* (e.g., *je parlons* 'we are speaking', noted above) is quite robust, occurring in almost 50% of tokens of first-person plural definite reference (Martineau 2005).[10] Interestingly, while these letters contain a number of narratives of personal experience, they do not contain any instances of the simple past. It must be kept in mind, then, that the enregisterment of dialect features in satirical texts should not be read as some faithful rendition or copy of language use in face-to-face interaction (see Agha 2003; Johnstone 2011).[11] Specific features inform what defines language varieties in such contexts, not the whole available repertoire.

There is a further complication with the Marichette text since: while Marichette describes herself in the letters as Nova Scotian, with brothers and sisters in New Brunswick and other relatives in the United States

(Gérin and Gérin 1982, 26), her actual identity was long a matter of debate and was not clearly resolved until Gérin and Gérin's examination of the existing evidence and their own interviews with living relatives. They conclude that Marichette was actually Emilie LeBlanc, born in Memramcooke, in southeastern New Brunswick, and that she was educated in a convent school there, attended (English-language) teacher's college in Fredericton, and only then spent several years as a teacher in Nova Scotia. As a chronicler of her times, a passionate Acadian and an early feminist, Marichette/ Emilie LeBlanc is an important figure in Acadian history. For our purposes, though, it would be wrong to view her writing as representative of Nova Scotia Acadian or as that of a semiliterate person, the author of choice for the linguistic study of informal letters.[12] Thus, while the Marichette texts are of interest for the indirect access they give to late-nineteenth-century Acadian usage, they are of limited use for reconstructing interdialectal variation of the period.

For all of the data sources, in the chapters that follow I pay close attention to the context in which linguistic variables are embedded. For instance, much has been made of the widespread use of *avoir* as an auxiliary in Acadian French, including with verbs of motion, such as *aller* 'to go', *retourner* 'to return', *descendre* 'to go down', and *venir* 'to come', along with verbs of state such as *rester* 'to stay' and even pronominal verbs such as *s'habiller* 'to dress oneself' (e.g., Giancarli 2011). With such verbs, Standard French would have *être* 'to be' as the auxiliary. If we return to Peacock's Newfoundland folksong corpus, we find usage such as the following, where *venir* 'to come' is indeed conjugated with *être* rather than *avoir*:

1. Dites-moi don', la belle, parlez-moi sans mentir
   Si vous êtes venues ici-e par force ou par plaisir.
   'Tell me then, beautiful one, speak to me without lying
   If you came here by force or by pleasure'
   [*Blanche comme la neige*, performed by Joséphine Costard, July 1959 (transcript, Peacock 1965, 174–75); my translation]

Compare the choice of auxiliary here, the second-person plural form of *être* (*vous êtes venues*), with that found in conversation between Mme. Le Costard and the linguist John Hewson in 1964, where only *avoir* 'to have' is found with the same verb, *venir*:[13]

2. JL: [Peacock] a pas venu depuis longtemps. Il avait boardé avec nous.
   JS: Oui, oui, couple de fois il a venu…
   JH: Ah oui?
   JL: Il a pas venu, il a pas venu back…[14]

JL: [Peacock] hasn't come for a long time. He had boarded with us.
JS: Yes, yes, couple of times he came…
JH: Oh yes?
JL: He hasn't come, he hasn't come back. [my translation]

This short excerpt contains, somewhat ironically, four tokens with *avoir* (*a (pas) venu*) in a discussion of Peacock's visit to Cap Saint-Georges. Since our sociolinguistic corpora for Newfoundland French show use of *être* with just two verbs, *mourir* 'to die' and *naître* 'to be born', a topic to which we will return in chapter 5, we may consider *avoir* the vernacular auxiliary par excellence in this variety. In this case, then, we see usage in ordinary discourse that is totally at odds with the performance of the folksong genre.

When we seek to compare, for example, the Newfoundland results with the published literature for other communities, we are sometimes perplexed as to whether there exists real intersystemic variation or whether differences seem to arise due to different analytic approaches. For instance, as Sankoff and Thibault (1980) observed in their groundbreaking study of auxiliary selection in Montreal French, it is not always clear whether particular data represent actions or states: *il est mort*, for instance, may indeed express the action 'he died', or it may describe the state 'he is dead'. In the first case, *est* is an auxiliary verb; in the second, it is a copula. While context often distinguishes auxiliaries from copulas, King and Nadasdi's (2005) study of auxiliary selection in Prince Edward Island French found fully 28% of all tokens (*n* = 203) to be ambiguous, as in the following example, presented here as three consecutive statements.

3. [*Il était*] *l'   homme   le   plus   fort   qu'   a   jamais*
   [he was]   the   man   the   more   strong   that   have.3SG.PRES   never
   *marché   à   Tignish.*
   walked   to   Tignish
   '[He was] the strongest man that ever walked to Tignish'

   *Il   est   mort.*
   he   be.3SG.PRES   died?/dead?
   'He died?/is dead?'

   *Il   s'   a   fait   mal.*
   he   REFL   have.3SG.PRES   made   ill
   'He hurt himself'

Here, as with many other tokens, the surrounding context does not enable us to determine whether or not the form of *être* is an auxiliary. I would argue that any study of auxiliary selection in French will likely have a considerable number of "don't count" tokens, of which the analyst should be aware.

However, for some linguists, especially those educated within particular French linguistic traditions, specific usages of *avoir* versus *être* may be analyzed as remnants of aspectual distinctions between the two whereby choice is affected by whether or not reference is being made to an action or result (for discussion, see Sankoff and Thibault 1980, 312–15). This notion seems to underlie Péronnet's (1975) description of southeastern New Brunswick usage, which perplexes the variationist-trained Marie-Marthe Roy in her own (1979) description of the same variety: where Péronnet sees auxiliary alternation, Roy sees near-categorical use of *avoir*. For Roy, much of Péronnet's *être* data are "don't count" cases involving copular constructions. The situation is complicated by the existence of an analytic tradition in explaining auxiliary alternation in French that is at odds with the variationist tradition of identifying the variable context: that is, from the latter perspective, processes but not states admit variation and only these should be counted.[15] I take Péronnet's and Roy's quite different descriptions of auxiliary selection to be symptomatic of this methodological difference rather than actual differences in the data they analyze.

I conclude this discussion of auxiliary selection by pointing to the same ambiguity presented by Henri Frei (1929, 104), a major source for early-twentieth-century vernacular Metropolitan French, also cited by Sankoff and Thibault. Frei's analysis is based in part on usage in a corpus of informal letters written by French soldiers during World War I.

One will note that "advanced" French, benefiting from the coexistence of two auxiliaries, *être* and *avoir*, in the past tense of intransitive verbs, tends to give distinct meanings according to which they involve the perfect ('state following a process': *être*) or the preterite ('process taking place in the past': *avoir*). [my translation][16]

What in fact was early-twentieth-century Metropolitan French like with respect to auxiliary alternation? Frei's short note is followed by several examples of intransitive verbs taking *avoir* (e.g., *revenir* 'to come back': *il na* [sic] *pas revenue à sa Cie depuis* 'he hasn't come back to his company since') but the one example of *être*, *il est mort*, is the same phrase in (3) above, deemed to be ambiguous. Without access to his letter corpus, Frei's comment may be interpreted only in light of unambiguous commentary and analysis for the period, or analysis of primary data. We return to auxiliary selection in chapter 5.

## COMPARATIVE METHODS

As the above discussion has indicated, the present work takes a comparative perspective. For example, while the varieties of French spoken in the province of Prince Edward Island have much in common with those spoken in the province of Newfoundland, there are also a number of properties they do not share. I focus on how such differences come about on the path of grammatical change. By looking at language use in communities that differ in the social context of spoken French, past and present, I track the role of social factors in language variation and change. By investigating substantial differences among varieties with closely related grammars, I test hypotheses about how particular grammatical properties are linked to one another.

The comparative method is, of course, standard to research in historical linguistics. As Tagliamonte (2002, 730) notes, its usefulness for sociolinguistic research was first recognized as part of the longstanding debates over the origins and development of African American Vernacular English. For instance, a number of contributers to Poplack's (2000) anthology on the origins of African American Vernacular English compare both rates of use and the relative importance of particular linguistic constraints for key variables in a number of varieties of English to show that African American varieties pattern much like earlier British varieties.[17] Other comparative sociolinguistic work has investigated patterns of variation at different points in time to determine whether there has been change in the grammatical system: a case in point is Leroux's (2005) study of change in the expression of past temporal reference in Quebec French. Leroux compares the past temporal reference system of Quebec French speakers born in the nineteenth and twentieth centuries, arguing that differences of constraint effects reflect change in the system across the generations.

Within the generative enterprise, a focus on the comparative syntax of "dialects" arguably crystallized in work on the structure of northern Italian varieties in the 1980s.[18] For instance, Brandi and Cordin (1989) suggest that in northern varieties, such as Trentino and Fiorentino, weak subject pronouns are not in fact subject clitic pronouns but agreement markers on the verb, an argument based in part on their quasi-obligatory nature, even in the presence of lexical subjects.[19] Facts about subject doubling (i.e., realization of the pronominal element along with a lexical subject or strong pronoun) in Italian led researchers to consider similar phenomena in varieties like Quebec French (Roberge 1990; Auger 1994) and European French vernaculars (Culbertson 2010): these varieties, too, are argued to pattern differently from Standard French, though it should be noted that this position has not been without its detractors (e.g., Côté 2001; De Cat 2005).

There is a clear impetus for this kind of comparative generative research, for as Rizzi (1989, 9) succinctly put it more than 20 years ago:

In the comparative study of dialects, we are dealing with very closely related grammatical systems, which differ only in a limited number of fundamental properties; these properties are thus relatively easy to isolate and to disentangle from any hidden interference. [my translation][20]

Study of the comparative syntax of Italian varieties in particular continues to flourish, as evidenced by recent publications by Ledgeway (2000) and D'Alessandro, Ledgeway, and Roberts (2010). Likewise, generative research on diachronic syntax can be seen to take a similar methodological approach in the comparison of different stages in the history of a language, for instance in works such as Lightfoot (2006) and Roberts (2007).

Some of my own research on Acadian French has combined both variationist and generativist perspectives. For instance, in explaining the linguistic trajectory of a very old borrowing in Acadian French, English-origin *back* (King 2000, 2011), I argue that in a number of varieties it has taken on the (syntactic and semantic) properties of an Acadian French aspectual adverb (e.g., *Tu as ti back fait?* should be translated as 'Did you do that again?'). I have also analyzed the use of orphan prepositions across varieties of North American French and the emergence of preposition stranding in some of those varieties from a combined variationist/formal perspective (King 2005a, 2011). I will draw on the research on prepositions as an illustration of the lexical diffusion of grammatical change in chapter 5. Likewise, a combined sociolinguistic/formal approach figures in my analysis of patterns of subject-verb agreement (King 2005b), to be taken up in chapter 4.

## DATA SOURCES FOR THIS BOOK

The data on which this study is based come first and foremost from large sociolinguistic corpora. These involve my own corpora and those of Gary R. Butler, to which I have kindly been granted access. The characteristics of these corpora are summarized in table 2.1.

The Newfoundland corpora comprise more than one million words from three communities, L'Anse-à-Canards, Cap Saint-Georges, and La Grand'Terre, and approximately 50,000 words for Stephenville/Kippens, where French was almost extinct when we recorded the last remaining speakers in 1980. The populations of these communities at the time of data

TABLE 2.1
Sociolinguistic Corpora Used for This Book

| Corpus | Date | No. | Corpus Creator | Interviewer(s) | Corpus Location | Interview Type |
|---|---|---|---|---|---|---|
| L'Anse-à-Canards, N.L. | 1978 | 10 | Ruth King | Ruth King | York Univ | socioling |
| L'Anse-à-Canards, La Grand'Terre, Cap-Saint-Georges, Stephenville/ Kippens, N.L. | 1980 | 68 | Ruth King | Ruth King | York Univ | socioling |
| Abram-Village, Tignish, P.E.I. | 1987 | 46 | Ruth King | community residents | York Univ | socioling |
| L'Anse–à-Canards, N.L. | 1988–89 | 20 | Gary Butler | community residents | York Univ | socioling |
| Grosses Coques, N.S. | 1989–90 | 31 | Gary Butler | community residents | York Univ | socioling |

collection in the 1980s was as follows: L'Anse-à-Canards, approximately 250; Cap Saint-Georges, approximately 950; La Grand'Terre, approximately 350; Kippens, approximately 1,200; and Stephenville, approximately 8,000.[21]

The Prince Edward Island corpus comprises 640,000 words, for two communities, Abram-Village and Saint-Louis. In addition, 8 child speakers were interviewed in Abram-Village, again by a community resident. These data are supplemented by 41 short recordings of artistic performances (mainly traditional folktales and community narratives) made by the folklorist Luc Lacourcière in the 1950s and 1960s.[22] At the time the corpus was constructed the population of Abram Village was approximately 350 while that of Tignish was around 150.

The Nova Scotia corpus, for the community of Grosses Coques in the Baie Sainte-Marie region, comprises 240,000 words. At the time the corpus was compiled, the population of Grosses Coques was approximately 1,200.

All of the late 1980s–early 1990s Acadian corpora involve the same (broad) set of interview questions and the same transcription protocol. In addition, I have relied on 79 short recordings of artistic performances made by the folklorist Luc Lacourcière, primarily in northeastern New Brunswick, in the 1950s and 1960s. Sociolinguistic interviews from Sylvie Dubois's Cajun French corpus (1997), supplemented by interviews conducted in the 1970s under the direction of Gerald Gold, Dean Louder, and Eric Waddell, were also consulted.[23] The interviews are for speakers born between 1890 and 1933 and include residents of Vermilion, Avoyelles, St. Landry, and Lafourche parishes.

For northeastern New Brunswick, I also draw on results of research on the Français acadien du nord-est du Nouveau Brunswick (FANENB-adultes) corpus, constructed under the direction of Louise Beaulieu in the early 1990s. The corpus comprises 100 hours of recordings of 16 speakers, interviewed by community insiders. Since this work involves variationist methodology and theorizing, comparisons with the results of my own research is fairly straightforward.

For southeastern New Brunswick, a number of small sociolinguistic corpora, particularly for adolescent speakers, exist, as research on this variety has virtually exploded since the early 1990s.[24] The documentation resulting from corpus-based work on these varieties includes a number of master's (e.g., Péronnet 1975; Roy 1979; Long 2008) and doctoral (e.g., Péronnet 1989b; Perrot 1995; Wiesmath 2000; Young 2002) theses. An earlier surge of interest in the Baie Sainte-Marie, Nova Scotia, variety resulted in doctoral theses by Gesner (1979a) and Ryan (1981), which give us access to the speech of elderly community residents of the period and provide good points of comparison with Péronnet's southeastern New Brunswick research in particular. They also provide good points of comparison with the Grosses Coques corpus.

The published literature also includes articles from the 1980s and 1990s by the sociolinguist Karin Flikeid, which are key to understanding the past history and present-day dynamics of Acadian varieties. Flikeid (1994) contextualizes late-twentieth-century linguistic variation in terms of the sociohistorical history of the Acadian people, while Flikeid and Péronnet (1989) provide detailed comparisons of New Brunswick and Nova Scotia varieties, in particular, the usage of elderly speakers. Along with these overview articles, I will draw from analyses of specific linguistic features of Acadian French found in the extant literature. To extend the time depth of the present research, at least for artistic performance, I will occasionally include data from the folklore recordings made in New Brunswick and Prince Edward Island by Luc Lacourcière, cited above.

For French Louisiana, I will rely largely on the published literature, in particular anthologies edited or coedited by Albert Valdman (e.g., Valdman, Auger, and Piston-Hatlen 2005), the sociolinguistic studies of Sylvie Dubois (1995) and Kevin Rottet (2001), and the recently published, authoritative *Dictionary of Louisiana French* (2010). In the Louisiana case, a number of early (1930s and 1940s) master's theses (e.g., Bernard 1933; Dugas 1935; Guilbeau 1936; Hickman 1940; Montgomery 1946) give us descriptions of usage in the early years of the twentieth century. In addition, the late-nineteenth-century folklorist Alcée Fortier provides early linguistic descriptions of Louisian varieties (e.g., Fortier 1891, 1894).

For comparative purposes, I will draw on data from the *Atlas linguistique de la France* (*ALF*) (Gilliéron and Édmont 1902–10), particularly for the source regions of Acadian settlement in the center-west of the country, as well as on French grammatical commentary across the centuries.[25] The *ALF* data were collected at the turn of the twentieth century from all across France and have longed served as an important point of comparion for twentieth-century (and beyond) dialectologists. However, it should be kept in mind that Gilliéron and Édmont sought out elderly informants deemed *patoisant*, that is, speakers of localized varieties believed to have developed during the medieval period, marked by mutual incomprehensibility. For example, for the center-west, they would have sought out speakers of varieties of Poitevin, Saintongeais, and the like rather than speakers of regional varieties of French.[26] As Flikeid (1994, 313) notes, twentieth-century decriptions of center-west patois show remarkably different morphology than one finds in Acadian varieties. Indeed, only certain phonetic features appear to be directly comparable. Regardless of whether or not we consider the original Acadian settlers to have been speakers of local patois or regional dialects, or some combination of both (a matter of some debate; see Flikeid 1994 in this regard), over 200 years separate Acadian settlement in the New World and the *ALF* data collection. Thus, comparison of the New World data with the rich source of information the *ALF* provides requires care and caution.

## VARIATION AND THE GRAMMAR(S)

In variationist sociolinguistics, there was remarkably little formal theoretical discussion of the status of variation and grammar from the 1980s to the 2000s, perhaps because functionalist approaches have dominated the variationist literature on grammatical variation and change since the 1980s. The work presented here is in the spirit of broadly generative approaches to language and is compatible with emerging trends in modeling morphosyntactic variation, or, put differently, with the emerging field of sociosyntax (Cornips and Corrigan 2005).

In my work I take as a starting point the construction of large sociolinguistic corpora, extraction of quantitative data for linguistic variables, and appropriate statistical testing. However, I view statistical testing as a means of hypothesis testing and do not consider the output of, say, multiple regression analysis as a direct reflection of linguistic competence (as in the "classic" 1970s conception of the variable rule). I do believe that variation can and should be modeled in a mental grammar: in current theory, Minimalist operations of feature interpretation and feature valuation can be used to build optionality into the grammar, an approach associated with David Adger and a number of others (e.g., Adger and Smith 2005; King 2005b; Adger 2006), which either integrates or is largely compatible with the theory of Distributed Morphology (Halle and Marantz 1993; Embick and Noyer 2007). Further, I follow the principle that grammatical change must be shown to be caused, in the sense of Longobardi (2001, 278–79):

[S]yntactic change should not arise, unless it can be shown to be *caused*—that is, to be a well-motivated consequence of other types of change (phonological changes and semantic changes, including the appearance/disappearance of whole lexical items) or, recursively, of other syntactic changes.... [Such an approach] forces us to look for explanations for all syntactic changes and to try to reduce unmotivated, primitive changes to the ineliminable minimum and, whenever possible, to find non–ad hoc explanations for this residue (e.g., on the grounds of independently observable external factors).

This approach puts a focus on both internal- and external-to-the-grammar sources of change and argues against both ad hoc and post hoc lines of explanation. Longobardi's approach is in line with that developed in my own work on grammatical borrowing (e.g., King 2000), from the same period.

In the following chapters, I will consider several cases of variation (and change) and take seriously the aim of modeling these results within a sociosyntactic perspective. Further, I will attempt to show how the ensemble of Acadian varieties involve similar grammars that differ from one another in clearly delineated ways.

# 3. A WINDOW ON THE PAST

THIS CHAPTER FOCUSES on the conservative nature of Acadian French, as shown by the survival of tense/aspect/mood distinctions lost in most other contemporary French varieties. I consider in particular the retention of rich verbal morphology in the simple tenses and its consequences for the grammars of the varieties in question.

In this and following chapters, I make use of both qualitative and quantitative analysis. I describe the manipulation and statistical analysis of the quantitative data—primarily through main effects logistical regression using the Goldvarb X statistical package (Sankoff, Tagliamonte, and Smith 2012)—so as to make the technical discussion as transparent as possible. Likewise, I introduce enough grammatical theory for the generalist to follow the analysis (e.g., I do not introduce any functional heads that are not "needed" for the description at hand) and enough information for the specialist to see the implications of a particular analysis.

## EARLY RESEARCH

In 1941, Ernest Haden, an American linguist from the University of Texas at Austin, made the first audio recording of an Acadian speaker telling a traditional folktale, *La Petite Cendrillouse*, an Acadian version of *Le Cendrillon* (Cinderella).[1] Moncton, New Brunswick, resident Jean-Thomas LeBlanc was a journalist for the French-language newspaper *L'Évangéline*, for which he published a column on traditional folksong. LeBlanc was not the typical older rural speaker favored by dialectologists of the period, but rather was an amateur folklorist.[2] However, he was clearly an enthusiast for all things Acadian. Haden's (1948) article presents a transcript of LeBlanc's performance of the folktale in eye dialect, a phonetic transcript of a small portion, and some notes on its linguistic characteristics. The recording itself sounds as if LeBlanc is reading a prepared text, albeit with much animation.[3]

The transcriptions contained in Haden's article based on this recording show the expected features of traditional Acadian phonology: including palatalization of /k/ and /g/ before non–low front vowels, as in interrogative *qui* [tʃi] 'who' and *guérir* [dʒerir] 'to heal'; preservation of aspirated /h/ in words like *dehors* 'outside'; and retention of [u] in words like *comme* [kum] 'like', where Standard French has [ɔ]—this last a phenomenon known as *ouisme* (Lucci 1972).[4] In terms of traditional lexicon, Haden (1948) supplies a list of 70-odd vocabulary items that he says do not correspond to "current" French usage. At the level of grammar, the text displays invariable use of auxiliary *avoir* 'to have', with no use of the *être* 'to be' auxiliary, a hallmark of Acadian usage unaffected by standard auxiliary alternation.[5]

Most notable for those interested in Acadian French grammar is LeBlanc's use of vernacular features long absent from the standard language and moribund in many dialects, both in Europe and North America by the mid-twentieth century. These include use of third-person plural verbal morphology in *-ont*, shown in (1) and (2):[6]

1. *Ces robes- là m' appartenont, je m'en*
   these dresses there me.DAT belong-3PL.PRES 1PERS REFL
   *vas les garder.*
   go.SG.PRES them keep-INF
   'These dresses belong to me, I am going to keep them'

2. *Elle a vu trois vieilles filles qu' étiont en frais de*
   she has seen three old girls who be-3PL.IMP in act of
   *faire l' ouvrage de la maison.*[7]
   do-INF the work of the house
   'She saw three old maids who were doing the housework'

This particular third-person plural variant was found even in literary French up until the sixteenth century but consigned to lower-class speech in France by the seventeenth century. In Europe, it was in decline in all but isolated rural varieties by the nineteenth century (King, Martineau, and Mougeon 2011). Thus, in most contemporary French varieties, regular verbs have a phonetically null ending in the third person, spelt *-ent*. However, in the LeBlanc version of the folktale, there are 50 unambiguous instances of the traditional variant and none at all of the -Ø variant.[8]

The text also shows categorical use of the subjunctive (*n* = 7) with subjunctive-selecting verbs (*vouloir* 'to want' and *souhaiter* 'to wish') and adverbial matrices (*avant que* 'before'), with use of the present subjunctive in (3) and (4) and the imperfect subjunctive in (5) and (6).

3. *Je veux que tous les filles, sans en manquer*
   1PERS want.SG.PRES that all the girls without PART miss-INF
   *une, veniont assayer le soulier.*[9]
   one come-3PL.PRES.SUBJ try-INF the shoe
   'I want all the girls, without exception, to come to try on the shoe'

4. *Je souhaite qu' elle ait trois robes.*
   1PERS wish.SG.PRES that she have.SG.PRES.SUBJ three dresses
   'I wish that she had three dresses'

5. *Le    roi    voulait        qu'   elle   allît             essayer   un   soulier*

    the    king   want-SG.IMP  that  she  go-SG.IMP.SUBJ  try-INF  a    shoe

    *que   son   garçon   avait            trouvé   sur  le    marche-pied  de*

    that  his   boy     have-SG.IMP  found  on   the   step          of

    *l'    église.*[10]

    the  church

    'The king wanted her to go try on a shoe that his son had found on the church step'

6. *Elle  a               couri  chus         eux   soigner        la*

    she  have.3SG.PRES  run    at.the.house.of  them  look.after-INF  the

    *maison  avant   que   son  père   et   la    Grousse  Laide  et    sa*

    house   before  that  her  father  and  the  big        ugly   and  her

    *mère     eurent           le   temps  d'  arriver.*[11]

    mother  have.PL.IMP.SUBJ  the  time   of  arrive-INF

    'She ran home to take care of the house before her father and the Wicked Stepmother and her mother had time to arrive'

The present subjunctive is, of course, still used in most varieties of spoken French, although some scholars (e.g., Poplack 1992) have argued that it does not serve any particular semantic function. The imperfect subjunctive, on the other hand, would have fallen into disuse in the spoken language from the Classical (i.e., seventeenth century) period on in the standard language (Fournier 1998).

There is also evidence of the simple past tense, shown in (7):

7. *Quand  la    Grousse  Laide  et    sa    mère    et   le    père   de*

    when   the  big     ugly   and  her  mother  and  the  father  of

    *la   Petite  Cendrillouse  se     rangirent     de     l'église,     la*

    the  little  Cinderella  REFL  go.back-PL.SP  from  the  church  the

    *Grousse  Laide  fut        à     la    Petite  Cendrillouse  qu'   avait*

    big       ugly   be.SG.SP  to   the  little   Cinderella   that  have-SG.IMP

    *v'nu   se     remettre      dans  le    coin   de  la    maison.*[12]

    came  REFL  back-put-INF  in     the   corner  of  the   house

    'When the Wicked Stepmother and Cinderella's father went back home from the church, the Wicked Stepmother went to Cinderella who had returned to the corner of the house'

Like the imperfect subjunctive, the French simple past is widely believed to have been lost in the spoken language by the turn of the nineteenth century. Indeed, the LeBlanc performance of the folktale suggests it may have not been in robust use in the southeastern New Brunswick Acadian variety of the period: even though the text is a narrative containing over 175 complicating action clauses, a context that has strongly favored the simple past in both speech and writing (see chapter 2), the vast majority of such clauses are rendered in the present perfect here; there are only 4 unambiguous simple past tokens.[13] Example (8), for instance, shows a sequence of complicating action clauses, all in the present perfect.

8. *Bientôt le roi a arrivé puis quand il a*
   soon the king have.3SG.PRES arrived and when he have.3SG.PRES
   *vu ça il a pris le rasoir puis il l'*
   seen that he have.3SG.PRES taken the razor and he it
   *a jeté là-bas.*
   have.3SG.PRES thrown over-there
   'Soon the king arrived and when he saw that, he took the razor and threw it aside'

Since (robust) use of the simple past has always been strongly linked to narration, as we saw earlier, the incursion of the present perfect here suggests that the system has been disrupted.

There are only two first-person plural tokens in the text, both contained in reported speech. Three variants of the first-person plural pronominal variable are attested in the history of French: *nous, on,* and *je.* From at least the Middle French period (fourteenth–fifteenth centuries), the subject pronoun *nous* was used in conjunction with the *-ons* verb ending, and the subject pronoun *je* was also in use accompanied by that same ending to indicate plural reference (Zink 1997, 335–36). The *je...ons* variant would follow the same trajectory as *ils...ont* in France (King, Martineau, and Mougeon 2011). Use of *on...Ø* with definite reference emerged somewhat later in the history of the language, after centuries of use with indefinite reference (similar to English indefinite *one*) and eventually supplanted both *je...ons* and *nous* even in spoken vernacular usage in France by the end of the nineteenth century. However, the LeBlanc text is not particularly useful for this variable, except that it documents variation in the system, as shown in examples (9) with *nous* and (10) with *on,* both taken from reported speeech.[14]

9. *Descendez icitte, nous filerons votre fil.*
   descend-2PL.IMPER here we spin-1PL.FUT your thread
   'Come down, we will spin your thread'
10. *Tandis qu' on filera ton fil tu balieras*
    while that one spin-3SG.FUT your thread you sweep.2SG.FUT
    *la place.*
    the floor
    'While we are spinning your thread, you will sweep the floor'

Only three future temporal reference tokens are found, all of them in the inflected (versus the periphrastic) future, as shown in (11) in reported speech. As we shall see below, the inflected future has been argued to be on the wane in both colloquial Metropolitan and Laurentian French for some time (Bauche 1920); a larger corpus is needed to investigate this claim in Acadian French, a topic to which we will return below.

11. *D'main      c'  est           toi   qui   iras          m'ner      les*
    tomorrow  it  be.3SG.PRES  you   who   go.2SG.FUT  lead-INF   the
    *vaches   au       parc.*
    cows     to.the   field
    'Tomorrow, it's you who will take the cows to the field'

On its own, then, the LeBlanc text gives us some insight into the structure of mid-twentieth-century Acadian French as spoken in the Moncton, New Brunswick, area. On the basis of its categorical use here, we may assume that *ils...ont* was a salient feature of Acadian French of the period. However, the text also raises a number of questions. We have no indication as to the status of *ils...ont*'s first-person plural counterpart, *je...ons*, in the variety. And while we find evidence of use of the simple past, unexpected in spoken mid-twentieth-century vernaculars, it seems to be vastly outclassed by the present perfect in what should be its prime context, narrative clauses involving complicating action. The imperfect subjunctive is likewise unexpected, but since there are few actual contexts in which it might occur in the text itself, we cannot hypothesize as to its status in the community. As for the expression of future temporal reference, the small amount of data is inconclusive.

All of these features—with the exception of third-person plural *ils...ont* and the expression of future temporal reference—would be noted by the French linguist and folklorist Geneviève Massignon, who, armed with a tape recorder and a bicycle, spent seven months in 1946 traversing Acadian regions of New Brunswick, Nova Scotia, and Prince Edward Island, along with parts of the province of Quebec.[15] Massignon's first published report on this fieldwork was a 1947 article in the American journal *The French Review*. As was noted in chapter 2, she describes "les parlers français de l'Acadie" as an ensemble with occasional mention of the particularities of specific regions. She does give a short folktale at the end of the article, collected from a Baie Sainte-Marie, Nova Scotia, resident in his 80s in 1947, thus giving us access, albeit limited, to language use of the second half of the nineteenth century.

If we do not limit ourselves to spoken language data, the historical record can be extended further back. Martineau (2005) studies grammatical variation in two satirical texts published toward the end of the nineteenth century, *Causerie memramcookienne* (published 1885–86 by the prolific Acadian writer, amateur linguist, and politician Pascal Poirier) and *Marichette: Lettres acadiennes 1895–1898*, written by the schoolteacher, Emily LeBlanc. In chapter 2, I discussed the status of such satirical texts for the reconstruction of nineteenth-century Acadian French: they are evidence of dialect enregisterment, though they may focus on some features but not others and also may lag behind the everyday use of the speech community. For the first-person plural variable, Martineau found 40.4% traditional usage ($n = 42$) in *Marichette* and 48.6% ($n = 142$) in *Causerie memramcookienne*. As for the third-person plural variable, both texts show very high rates of traditional usage, 99.3% ($n = 165$) for *Marichette* and 81.5% ($n = 33$) for *Causerie*.[16] Since both Poirier and LeBlanc were natives of southeastern New Brunswick, we will contrast these results to the later historical record for the variety. Based on 1970s fieldwork in this area, both Péronnet (1989a, 1989b) and Roy (1979) attest that *je...ons* is found only in the speech of the very old—in Roy's case, in the speech of an 89-year-old at the time of 1976 fieldwork—whereas *ils...ont* does not have this restriction. Tellingly, *je...ons* is not even part of the set of enregistered features for this variety found in satirical texts from the early twentieth century (Comeau and King 2011).[17] We cannot, however, pinpoint exactly when these features actually went into serious decline in the southeastern New Brunswick variety.

## THE CONSERVATIVE SYSTEM

Table 2 presents paradigms for the simple tenses (present indicative, preterite, and inflected future, along with the imperfect, conditional, and the present and imperfect subjunctives) in conservative varieties of Acadian French. These distinctions are all present in the variety of Baie Sainte-Marie, Nova Scotia, Acadian spoken in the village of Grosses Coques and represented by data in the sociolinguistic corpus for this community. As was noted in chapter 2, Baie Sainte-Marie is home to the most conservative of Acadian varieties, preserving a number of features lost in the Acadian French of, say, southeastern New Brunswick. We may thus take it as a baseline for comparison with other present-day varieties.

Table 2 shows that the third-person singular and plural are always distinct in traditional varieties; thus, the data show a contrast in place at the time of seventeenth-century immigration to the New World. Further, we see that first-person singular *je...ons* is in use, a form now largely lost from other spoken French varieties. We also see that the inflected future is

TABLE 3.1
Acadian French Simple Tenses (Conservative Varieties)

|  | *Present Indicative* | *Simple Past* | *Imperfect* | *Conditional* |
|---|---|---|---|---|
| Singular |  |  |  |  |
| 1st person | je parle | je parlis | je parlais | je parlerais |
| 2nd person | tu parles | tu parlis | tu parlais | tu parlerais |
| 3rd person | il/elle/ça parle | il/elle/ça parlit | il/elle/ça parlait | il parlerait |
| Plural |  |  |  |  |
| 1st person | je parlons | je parlirent | je parlions | je palerions |
| 2nd person | vous parlez | vous parlirent | vous parliez | vous parleriez |
| 3rd person | ils parlont | ils parlirent | ils parliont | ils parleriont |

|  | *Simple Future* | *Present Subjunctive* | *Imperfect Subjunctive* |
|---|---|---|---|
| Singular |  |  |  |
| 1st person | je parlerai | je parle | je parlis |
| 2nd person | tu as parleras | tu parles | tu parlis |
| 3rd person | il/elle/ça parlera | il/elle/ça parle | il/elle/ça parlit |
| Plural |  |  |  |
| 1st person | je parlerons | je parlions | je parlirent |
| 2nd person | vous parlerez | vous parliez | vous parlirent |
| 3rd person | ils parleront | ils parliont | ils parlirent |

retained, a form which a number of twentieth-century European commentators have argued is losing ground to the periphrastic future in the spoken language (we turn to the inflected variant's relationship to the periphrastic variant below). Also included is the simple past, object of earlier discussion in this chapter and in chapter 2, along with the imperfect subjunctive.[18] As has been noted by numerous commentators, the three conjugations of the simple past (maintained in written Standard French) were replaced by two in vernacular French by the sixteenth century at least: the <a> and <i> conjugations have fallen together, giving an <i> rather than standard French <a> conjugation with -*er* verbs (see Lodge 2004 and Chauveau 2009 for discussion).

For the simple past and the imperfect subjunctive, we find homophonous plural endings where Standard French would have, for <i> conjugation verbs, first-person plural -*îmes*, second-person plural -*îtes*, and third-person plural -*irent*. Note that in Acadian varieties that retain the simple past, <u> conjugation verbs likewise have -*urent* throughout the plural paradigm, rather than distinct forms for each person. The question arises as to whether these analogical formations are specific to Acadian French. For instance, the regularized forms are not found in theatrical representations of lower-class speech from the seventeenth century (e.g., the parodic dialogues contained in *Les Mazarinades*, the works of playwrights like Molière, etc.). In grammars of center-west dialects (more technically, *patois* in the French tradition), we do find plural forms with [ir] but there is also subject (person) agreement as well. For instance, Svenson's (1959) grammar for Marais-Vendée gives the following conjugation for *donner* 'to give':[19]

First-person singular: duɲi[1]
Second-person singular: duɲi
Third-person singular: duɲit
First-person plural: duɲiraŋ
Second-person plural: duɲirɛɪ
Third-person plural: duɲirɑt

In the *Atlas linguistique de la France*, use of the present perfect far surpasses that of the simple past, but where there is (variable) usage, one finds forms like those given in Svenson, particularly in the center-west, as shown, for example, in map 1154, for which the target sentence was *nous le revîmes plus* 'we didn't see him any more'.[20] One does find usage like that in table 3.1, without person agreement (see points 25 and 58). Since these particular villages are somewhat removed from the center-west, we can only conclude that the Acadian French forms have European French parallels, but whether or not they have been retained from source varieties in France or are New World innovations is unknown.[21]

The system which underlies table 3.2 involves much richer overt morphology than does Standard French and most contemporary varieties.[22] We will first consider the extent to which this morphology is preserved in different Acadian varieties by making cross-dialectal quantitative comparisons for the first-person plural and third-person plural variables. Table 3.2 presents a set of proportional comparisons. The data presented for four Nova Scotia communities (i.e., all but Grosses Coques) and for southeastern New Brunswick come from Flikeid and Péronnet's (1989) cross-varietal comparison of usage of eight older speakers for each of the five regions. The Grosses Coques, Newfoundland, and Prince Edward Island data come from similar speaker samples. The northeastern New Brunswick data come from Beaulieu's FANENB corpus (the entire speaker sample, reported on in Beaulieu and Cichocki 2008). The Louisiana data come from 64 older speakers representative of four Cajun parishes, drawn from Dubois's 1997 Louisiana French corpus and from Gold, Louder, and Wadell's 1970s Cajun French corpus. Although the samples are not uniform, we are still able to tease apart differences, as well as similarities, in usage.

First note that L'Anse-à-Canards, Newfoundland, and Grosses Coques, Nova Scotia, have proportions of both traditional variants that approach categoriality: these are arguably varieties that have been least influenced by supralocal varieties. Grosses Coques has a relatively heterogeneous settle-

TABLE 3.2
Frequency of *je* + Verb + *-ons* and *ils* + Verb + *-ont* in Several Acadian Varieties

| Communities | je + Verb + -ons | ils + Verb + -ont |
|---|---|---|
| Grosses Coques, N.S. | 99 | 99 |
| L'Anse-à-Canards, N.L. | 97 | 99 |
| Saint-Louis, P.E.I. | 76 | 83 |
| Abram-Village, P.E.I. | 18 | 78 |
| Île-Madame, N.S. | 83 | 78 |
| Pubnico, N.S. | 60 | 73 |
| Pomquet, N.S. | 75 | 87 |
| Chéticamp, N.S. | 59 | 84 |
| Meteghan, N.S. | 59 | 72 |
| Southeast N.B. | very low | 70 |
| Northeast N.B. | — | 20 |
| Louisiana (4 parishes) | — | 16 |

SOURCES: Flikeid and Péronnet (1989); Dubois, Nadasdi, and King (2004); King, Nadasdi, and Butler (2004); King (2005); Comeau and King (2006); Beaulieu and Cichocki (2008).

ment history and is located in the area of Nova Scotia with the highest concentration of Acadians. L'Anse-à-Canards has had a more diverse settlement history but remained in virtual isolation from other francophone groups and in considerable isolation from English until well into the second half of the twentieth century. Although L'Anse-à-Canards has lost the simple past, the reasons for which I will consider below, this variety has proven conservative on any number of measures in prior research (King and Butler 2005).[23]

While Abram-Village and Saint-Louis, Prince Edward Island, are about an hour's drive from one another, there is a world of difference between the two communities, as was noted in chapter 2. Abram-Village enjoys considerable institutional support for French and is a summer tourist destination for Quebec residents. The split between the two communities with respect to diminished use of one of the two traditional variants, first-person plural *je... ons*, is not unexpected. However, in all but two of the Acadian communities, third-person plural *ils... ont* is in robust use, in some cases considerably more robust than its first-person plural counterpart. We might well ask what it is about *je... ons* that makes it the first of the two traditional variants to weaken? King, Nadasdi, and Butler (2004) attempt to answer this question in their study of the split between the two Prince Edward Island varieties: they suggest that this discrepancy occurs because the contrast between the vernacular and nonvernacular forms is more marked in the first-person plural than in the third-person plural. A comparison of the two cases shows that what differentiates the two variables is that the first-person variable involves a change in pronominal clitic along with loss of a suffix on the verb (e.g., *je parlons* vs. *on parle*), while the third-person case involves (uniquely) loss of the suffix (e.g., *ils parlont* vs. *ils parlent*, recall that *-ent* is phonetically null). Further, the retention of the *-ont* suffix in the third-person plural may be reinforced by the occurrence in the standard language and in other vernaculars of high-frequency irregular verbs with *-ont*, such as *aller* 'to go' > *ils vont*, *être* 'to be' > *ils sont*, and *avoir* 'to have' > *ils ont*. The fact that the first-person plural vernacular variant is highly distinctive, providing a marked contrast with the *on* variant, seems the motivation for its strong association with local norms and its potential for reevaluation, often as a stigmatized variant.[24]

This appears to be the case in southeastern New Brunswick, where Martineau and Tailleur's (2011) study of informal letters written between 1893 and 1928 by members of an extended family from southeastern New Brunswick and their relatives in Massachussetts provide an early data source for Acadian French. While *ils…ont* accounts for nearly half of the first-person plural data, *je…ons* proves to be a minority variant, used in 11% of cases. It would appear, then, that *je…ons* may be targeted while *ils…ont* flies under the radar. Thus, it is not surprising that Flikeid and Péronnet (1989), like Roy (1979) before them, found *je…ons* to be used only by very old Moncton-area speakers: in fact, only one of their eight older southeast speakers was a *je…ons* user. A similar diminished usage of *je…ons* appears to have taken place in the Îles de la Madeleine: while Hubert (1938) finds widespread usage of this variant, Falkert's (2005) study based on her 2003 corpus for 30 speakers found *je…ons* to be very nearly extinct.

Not surprisingly, *je…ons* is entirely absent from Beaulieu's 100-hour corpus for northeastern New Brunswick. In fact, its disappearance is foreshadowed by Geddes's (1908, 115) remarks based on his 1890 fieldwork in Carleton, Baie des Chaleurs:

[T]he use of dialect *ɔ̃(n)* for Fr. *nous* is Carleton usage, my notes in other Acadian districts lead me to believe that it is not Acadian but decidedly Canadian and is here due to Canadian influence. The Acadian usage […] can be heard, tho rarely in Carleton, for I have recorded *ʒ avjɔ̃* = j'avions; *ʒ etjɔ̃* = j'étions.

In fact, in the northeast the proportion of *ils…ont* also falls dramatically in Beaulieu's early 1990s corpus. However, Beaulieu and Cichocki (2008) report that this latter variant is still used to some degree by speakers with closed social networks (Milroy 1980) and serves as a marker of in-group membership.

## TWO VARIETIES, TWO OUTCOMES

The reader may well ask at this point what the verbal paradigms for north-eastern New Brunswick and Cajun Louisiana actually look like. While they resemble each other in that there is much less overt verbal morphology (e.g in both cases *je...ons* is absent and *ils...ont* is decidedly a minority variant) than is the case for the other Acadian varieties reported on in table 3.2, they are dramatically different from each other. We will consider each in turn.

Table 3.3 gives the verbal paradigm for northeastern New Brunswick French presented in Beaulieu and Balcom's (1998) article on the status of subject pronouns in this variety. This table shows that northeastern New Brunswick French is just like most present-day French varieties in that only the second-person plural always shows a distinct inflectional ending; it dif-fers from, say, vernacular Laurentian French in that *ils...ont* is a minority third-person plural variant.[25] We see also that *il* and *ils* may reduce to [i] or [j] regardless of following phonological environment, whereas in a more conservative variety like Newfoundland Acadian, *l*-deletion is phonologi-cally conditioned: the /l/ is typically absent before consonants (King 1983). The verbal paradigm is thus quite different from the one presented in the previous table.[26]

Table 3.4 presents the verbal paradigm for the Louisiana Cajun variety spoken in Terrebonne and Lafourche Parishes in the coastal marsh area of southeastern Louisiana, as presented in Rottet's (2001, 144) study of lan-guage shift. Table 3.4 is somewhat deceptive in that it resembles table 3.3 since there is a clear reduction in verbal endings, as compared to the con-

TABLE 3.3
The Verbal Paradigm for Northeastern New Brunswick French
(adapted from Beaulieu and Balcom 1998)

| Person/Number | Regular Verb Conjugation | Subject Marker | Verbal Ending |
|---|---|---|---|
| 1st-person singular | j'arrive | je~j | Ø |
| 2nd-person singular | tu arrives | tu~t | Ø |
| 3rd-person singular | | | |
|    masculine | /j/ arrive | i~/j/ | Ø |
|    feminine | al~a arrive | al~a | Ø |
| 1st-person plural | on arrive | on | Ø |
| 2nd-person plural | vous arrivez | vous | /e/ |
| 3rd-person plural | | | |
|    masculine | /j/ arrivent | i~/j/ | Ø |
|    feminine | /j/ arrivont | | /õ/ |

TABLE 3.4

The Verbal Paradigm for Terrebonne-Lafourche Cajun French

(Rottet 2001)

| Person/Number | Regular Verb Conjugation | Verbal Ending |
|---|---|---|
| 1st-person singular | je parle | Ø |
| 2nd-person | | |
| informal | tu parles | Ø |
| formal | vous parlez[a] | /e/ |
| 3rd-person singular | | |
| masculine | il parle | Ø |
| feminine | elle parle | Ø |
| 1st-person plural | on parle | Ø |
| 2nd-person plural | vous-autres parle | Ø |
| 3rd-person plural | | |
| masculine | ils parlont | Ø |
| feminine | ils, ça, eusse, eux-autres parle | |

a. Highly restricted in use.

servative Acadian case. However, the system here is also marked by use of strong pronominal forms (*vous-autres, eusse < eux*, and *eux-autres*) along with infrequent use of the *vous* pronoun.[27] Other Cajun French sources also suggest that the one verbal ending in this table is being lost: Ditchy (1932) cites forms such *vous va* 'you go' and *vous veut* 'you want', with singular forms of the verb co-occurring with *vous*. Conwell and Juilland (1963) likewise record *vous connais* 'you know' and *vous sait* 'you know'.[28] Dubois, King, and Nadasdi's (2004) study of third-person plural usage in the speech of 64 consultants from four parishes who were born no later than 1933 found only 16% of tokens (*n* = 2,098) used the traditional *-ont* morphology (this is the source of the figure given in table 3.2). Of these traditional morphology tokens, all but 9 co-occur with the pronoun *ils*: that is, there was virtually no morphological marking on the verb with a strong pronominal form such as *eusse* or with a lexical subject. Further, Lafourche Parish, which stands out in its preservation of phonetic variants strongly linked to Acadian French, such as [ʃ] *saintongeais*, has arguably lost the *-ont* inflectional ending since Lafourche speakers in the sample provided only 4 of 252 tokens with this ending.[29] As for the *je...ons* variant of the first-person plural, it is attested in Ditchy's (1932) turn-of-the-twentieth-century grammatical sketch but appears to have disappeared in the early twentieth century.[30]

Another clue as to the nature of the verbal system is found in how Louisiana varieties treat borrowed verbs. In all other French varieties of which I am aware, including European French, borrowed verbs of English origin are morphologically incorporated into French (e.g., Acadian *starter* (infinitive), *starté* (past participle). In the Prince Edward Island corpus, for instance, all but one of the thousands of verb tokens produced by fluent French speakers occurred with the appropriate French morphological marking, regardless of frequency in the corpus. On the other hand, Louisiana French verbs of English origin are not morphologically integrated at all. Whereas English 'He has retired (from his job)' is rendered *il a retiré* in Atlantic Canada Acadian French, with the French past participle marker attached to the stem, in Louisiana French varieties one has simply *il a retire* [riytayr] (example from Brown 1986; see also Picone 1993; Dubois and Sankoff 1996). Picone provides examples that show bare infinitival forms, as in *il voulait check sur la situation* where Atlantic Canada varieties would have *checker.*

Finally, I note the plethora of strong pronoun forms in the table where the other French varieties would have clitic pronouns. We do find limited use of strong pronouns in other varieties of French, particularly in the third-person singular, for stylistic effect (Jones 1996, 250). Example (12) contains an example from the L'Anse-à-Canards, Newfoundland, corpus, which involves constrast.

> 12. *Eusse parliont plus anglais que nous-autres.*
>     them speak-3PL.IMP more English than us-others
>     'They used to speak more English than us'

I have argued elsewhere that such usage in the Newfoundland varieties is actually a throwback to usage in earlier stages of the language (King and Nadasdi 1997): it typically involves contrast but between second-person *toi* and third-person plural *eusse* as well as third-person masculine singular *lui.*[31] However, in the third-person plural Louisiana study, strong pronouns accounted for nearly 10% of the data and did not appear to be stylistically marked in any way. These data, in fact, point to the loss of verbal morphology, and to the erosion of the clitic pronoun system, the latter having begun in the third person.

## THE EXPRESSION OF FUTURE TEMPORAL REFERENCE

Thus far we have considered variable usage in a rather limited way, having calculated proportions of traditional usage for first- and third-person plural. However, along with relative frequency, we also want to know how usage is constrained. Specifically, a leading question of diachronic variationist research is whether or not constraints known to have been in effect for earlier stages of the language are still operative. A case in point is the expression of future temporal reference in French, the object of much quantitative research in recent decades. Specifically, studies of Laurentian French (e.g., Deshaies and Laforge 1981; Emirkanian and Sankoff 1985; Poplack and Turpin 1999; Poplack and Dion 2009; Grimm and Nadasdi 2011; Wagner and Sankoff 2011) have found that factors long associated with choice of the inflected versus the periphrastic future today exhibit weak or nonexistent effects and that one particular factor, sentential polarity, hardly mentioned as a conditioning factor in the documentation on the history of the language, is the predictor of variant choice par excellence. The periphrastic future dominates in (highly frequent) affirmative contexts, whereas (relative infrequent) negative contexts seem to be the last bastion of the inflected future.

If Acadian varieties do present a kind of window on the past, they should line up with what has been documented for earlier stages of the language.[32] King and Nadasdi's (2003) study of the expression of future temporal reference in Prince Edward Island and Newfoundland French provides the primary test case. Examples (13)–(15) show the three main variants for the expression of future temporal reference: the inflected future (13), the periphrastic future (14), and the futurate present (15). These examples are all taken from the Butler Sociolinguistic Corpus for L'Anse-à-Canards.

13. *Je      crois           bien   qu'  ils    boiront        ailleurs.*
    1PERS believe.SG.PRES well  that  they   drink-3PL.FUT elsewhere
    'I think that they will drink elsewhere'

14. *Je      m'en  vas    t'arranger une  tasse, une  belle    tasse  de  cocoa*
    1PERS REFL  you   fix-INF    a    cup   a    lovely  cup   of  cocoa
    *chaud,  ça    va    te     faire        du     bien.*[33]
    hot     that  go.SG you    make-INF     some   good
    'I'm going to make you a cup, a lovely cup of hot cocoa, it is going to do you good'

15. *Asteure comme Daddy, il   sait           en  masse des histoires aussi.*
    now     like  daddy  he   know.SG.PRES a   lot   of  stories   too
    *Si il y     aurait          moyen de  toutes les   écrire    en   bas,*
    if  there have.SG.COND  way   of  all   them  write-INF in   below
    *tu  sais   hein, comme  ça,   ils   sont          pas perdus hein.*[34]
    you know   eh    like   that  they  be.3PL.PRES  NEG lost    eh
    'Now like Daddy, he knows lots of stories, too. If there were a way of writing them down, you know, eh, like that, they are not lost, eh' [AC-3]

Note that an important step in preparing a corpus for quantitative analysis of the expression of future temporal reference is ridding the data set of so-called "false futures," such as the highly frequent use of future morphology to express habitual actions, as exemplified in (16).[35]

16  C' était      étrange   parce    c' est              pas      souvent  qu'
    it be.SG.IMP  strange   because  it be.3SG.PRES NEG  often    that
    une personne  va        rêver    du      bon    Jésus.
    a    person   go.SG.PRES dream-INF of.the good   Jesus
    'It was strange because it's not often that a person is going to dream about Jesus'

The importance of this step cannot be overemphasized. For instance, Wagner and Sankoff (2011) found that fully 45% of their data involving periphrastic future forms consisted of the expression of habituality, not future temporal reference.

Table 3.5 shows substantial use of the inflected future in all three Acadian varieties under study. In comparison, studies of Laurentian French have results ranging from a low of 12% (Grimm and Nadasdi 2011, Hawkesbuy, ON 1978 corpus) to a high of 22% (Poplack and Turpin 1999, Ottawa-Hull 1982 corpus).[36] It is important to keep in mind, though, that the Acadian study focused on older speakers, as did the studies of first- and third-person pronominal choice: that is, the study centered on the conservative system in place, rather than degree of retention by younger generations. As we shall see below, this lacuna has been filled by more recent work.

The potential conditioning factors on how future temporal reference is expressed include temporal reference, or proximity to the speech event. Indeed, the French periphrastic future is often called the *future proche*, or near future. We hypothesized that the nearer the event is to the moment of speech, the more likely the periphrastic future is used; this is the major conditioning factor enshrined in traditional grammars of the language. The literature also suggests that the more certain an event is to take place, the more likely the periphrastic future is used; the inflected future, on the other hand, is associated with psychological distance, or neutrality. Events contingent upon another event have been argued to favor the inflected

TABLE 3.5
Overall proportion of the Inflected Future in Three Acadian French Varieties
(adapted from King and Nadasdi 2003)

| Community | No. of Speakers | Proportion of Inflected Futures |
|---|---|---|
| L'Anse-à-Canards, N.L. | 8 | 40% |
| Saint-Louis, P.E.I. | 8 | 57% |
| Abram-Village, P.E.I. | 8 | 59% |

future and, in communities where the inflected future has been reanalyzed as a formal variant, there is a strong association with use of formal *vous*. However, in studies of Laurentian French, polarity exerts the strongest conditioning effect on variation: while grammarians and commentators rarely mention such an influence, and indeed there is no consensus among linguists as to why there should be such an effect, the inflected future is primarily associated with negation. This is the finding of all of the studies of Laurentian French noted above.[37]

Following standard practice, the data were submitted to main effects multiple regression analysis using the Goldvarb statistical package. In the presentation of results in table 3.6, factor weights measure the relative effects of sets of factors (factor groups) on variation. A factor weight may range between 0 and 1, with factor weights below .5 exhibiting a disfavoring effect on use and above .5 a favoring effect. The results are presented from the perspective of relative use of the periphrastic future, which, in other words, provides the application (input) value.

In light of the findings of previous quantitative studies, the results in table 3.6 are striking. First, note that temporal reference strongly affects choice of the periphrastic versus inflected future: in these Acadian varieties, we are really dealing with a *futur "proche"* in that events within a week of the moment of speech favor this variant. Likewise, certainty behaves in the predicted way: more certain events are rended with the periphrastic future.

TABLE 3.6
Effects of Potential Conditioning Factors on the Expression
of Future Temporal Reference in Acadian French
(application [input] value = periphrastic future; King and Nadasdi 2003)

| Factor Groups | Factor Weights | N | |
|---|---|---|---|
| Temporal Reference | | | |
| within hour | .69 | 70/90 | (78%) |
| within day | .68 | 36/50 | (72%) |
| within week | .65 | 35/49 | (42%) |
| longer than a week | .48 | 176/442 | (40%) |
| continual | .14 | 6/54 | (11%) |
| *Range* | 55 | | |
| Certainty | .69 | 178/246 | (72%) |
| | .39 | 145/349 | (33%) |
| *Range* | 30 | | |

NOTE: Factor groups not selected as significant: adverbial specification, contingency, grammatical person, polarity.

Contrary to what has been found for Laurentian varieties, polarity does not influence variant choice. This is an important finding as it lends support to the idea that polarity is a relatively recent constraint on the expression of future temporal reference in French: it does not emerge as significant in our "window on the past."

The variationist reader may ask at this point if these same results would be true had we considered wider age ranges for each of the three Acadian communities considered here: recall that the aim of King and Nadasdi (2003) was not to investigate possible change in the system, or systems, but to tap the speech of older residents. In fact, Comeau (2011) replicates our previous work in two Baie Sainte-Marie Acadian communities, Grosses Coques and Meteghan: unlike our 2003 study, Comeau's study considers a wide age range. It turns out that Comeau found the same robust use of the inflected future that we had found, along with temporal reference as the main and strongest factor group conditioning variation. Equally important, polarity was not selected as significant. There was also no age effect; that is, there was no evidence that the system is undergoing change. This is not to say that I assume that all Acadian varieties would have similar results: there is no comparable work on future temporal reference in northeastern New Brunswick French, spoken near the Quebec border, nor has such a study been carried out in the Louisiana context. For different reasons in each case (see previous section), we might expect reduced levels of the inflected future in these speech communities.

## PAST TEMPORAL REFERENCE

In a similar vein, Comeau, King, and Butler (2012) analyze the expression of past temporal reference in Baie Sainte-Marie, Nova Scotia, French. The three main ways of expressing temporal reference in French are illustrated in 18 (with the verb in the imperfect), 19 (present perfect), and 20 (simple past).[38] The data come from the Grosses Coques corpus.

18. *Je    lui    parlis    un    élan,    là.*
    1PERS him-DAT speak-SG.SP a while there
    'I spoke to him for a while'
19. *J'    ai    point parlé    trop longtemps.*
    1PERS have.1SG.PRES NEG spoke too long
    'I didn't speak too long'
20. *Elle se    parlait    toute seule, steady.*
    she REFL speak-SG.IMP all alone steady
    'She used to talk to herself, all the time'

The Grosses Coques sample for this particular study comprised 14 speakers, ranging from young adult to elderly, with an equal number of males and females. Table 3.7 shows an almost even split between the imperfect and the present perfect in the data, along with a sizable number of simple past tokens, accounting for 20% of the data. The simple past was strongly present in the speech of all consultants: as in the case of the future temporal reference variable, no social factors emerged as significant in the quantitative analysis. Additional evidence of the productive nature of this tense is its use of verbs of English origin, as in (21).

21. *Il    se    levit.*        *Il    divit* [daɪvi]  *la    tête    là    première   dans*
    he   REFL  get.up-SG.SP    he   dive-SG.SP    the   head   there  first      in
    *la    place.*
    the   floor
    'He got up. He dove headfirst onto the floor'

While table 3.7 shows evidence for overall robust use of the simple past in the Grosses Coques corpus, table 3.8 presents the results for constraints on its use.[39] As in the case of the future temporal reference variable, a number of potential conditioning factors were selected from the literature for testing: these include temporal distance from the moment of speech, sentential and lexical aspect, presence of adverbial specification, subject type, and priming effects. With respect to temporal difference, the data were coded for Estienne's (1578) famous "24-hour" rule, the sixteenth-century grammarian's attempt to specifiy the degree of remoteness involved in choice of the simple past versus the present perfect: he allowed that events occurring more than 24 hours prior to the moment of speech should be rendered in the former and less than 24 hours before that moment in the latter. Given the fact that many commentators and linguists have associated use of the simple past with narration (e.g., Benveniste 1959), the data were also coded for discourse mode, specifically whether they involved narration or conversation. All clauses were thus coded as narrative versus nonnarrative, and, following Labov and Waletzky (1967) and Labov (1997), each narrative clause was identified by structural type: abstract, orientation, com-

TABLE 3.7

Overall Results for Past Temporal Reference in Grosses Coques French
(Comeau, Butler, and King 2013)

| | | |
|---|---|---|
| Imparfait | 1,128 | (39%) |
| Passé Composé | 1,242 | (41%) |
| Passé Simple | 575 | (20%) |

TABLE 3.8

Effects of Potential Conditioning Factors on the Expression
of Past Temporal Reference
(application [input] value = simple past; Comeau, King, and Butler 2012)

| *Factor Groups* | *Factor Weights* | *N* | |
|---|---|---|---|
| Discourse Mode | | | |
| narrative (complicating action) | .92 | 451/556 | (82%) |
| narrative (other clause types) | .72 | 49/108 | (45%) |
| conversation | .19 | 74/1,038 | (7.1%) |
| *Range* | 71 | | |
| Adverbial Specification | | | |
| no adverbial specification | .53 | 525/1,401 | (37%) |
| time specification | .36 | 56/279 | (20%) |
| duration specification | .32 | 3/22 | (14%) |
| *Range* | 21 | | |
| Sentential Aspect | | | |
| punctual | .55 | 495/1,191 | (42%) |
| habitual/durative combined | .38 | 79/511 | (16%) |
| *Range* | 17 | | |

NOTE: Factor not selected: subject type.

plicating action, coda, or evaluation. In the Labovian tradition, a narrative is defined structurally as a sequence of clauses which follows "the basic rule of narrative sequencing […], which allow the listener to infer the reported temporal order to past events from the temporal sequence of clauses in the report of those events" (Labov 1982, 225). Thus, we identify narrative clauses as those whose temporal order may not be switched without changing the chronological order of events.

The results in table 3.8 represent the best model of variation based on a series of independent Goldvarb runs. This procedure was necessary since several of the potential conditioning factors mentioned above interact with one another: for instance, discourse mode interacts with temporal distance since events only become "tellable" as narrative only after a certain amount of time has passed. This results in very few narrative tokens in data describing events taking place within 24 hours of the moments of speech. To take another example, discourse mode also interacts with sentential aspect since complicating action clauses are overwhelmingly punctual. Since the Goldvarb package assumes independence of factor groups, they were run in different combinations so that interacting factor groups were never combined in a single run.

The results in table 3.8 show that the simple past is overwhelmingly associated with narration, in particular with complicating action clauses. This does not mean that temporal distance from the moment of speech is not important or relevant, but rather that the results for discourse mode, which closely correspond to temporal distance in the data set, provide the best "fit" (in statistical terms) to the data. We can, then, interpret these results as yet another demonstration of the conservative nature of the Baie Sainte-Marie variety. The appendix contains three narratives of personal experience that exemplify the structure of tense/aspect variation in this variety.

Flikeid and Péronnet (1989) looked briefly at the homophonous simple past and imperfect subjunctive in their cross-dialectal study of grammatical variation in Acadian French, as I noted above. While they did not do full-scale quantitative analysis, distinguishing the two usages for all of their data, they did determine whether or not the simple past was part of individual speakers' repertoires. For New Brunswick, they found no unambiguous simple past tense usage, although there were clear tokens for the imperfect subjunctive (i.e., they were found in subjunctive-selecting contexts). We do not know for certain, but by the mid-twentieth century, simple past usage (see Haden 1948) may have been limited to artistic genres in southeastern New Brunswick; Geddes (1908, 274) states that neither the simple past nor the imperfect subjunctive was found in the northeast in the late nineteenth century.[40] Interestingly, in Flikeid and Péronnet's Nova Scotia data, the most educated speakers seemed to be avoiding the simple past tense, in particular the plural forms in -irent and -urent, which, in the first- and second-person plural, depart dramatically from Standard French (written) usage, as we have seen. Thus, the simple past turns out to pattern like je... ons, in that it is quite salient and sensitive to correction.

I have investigated use of the simple past quantitatively only in the Grosses Coques corpus since in my other corpora one finds only sporadic (Prince Edward Island) use of this tense or indeed it is not even attested (L'Anse-à-Canards, N.L.). Now while the Abram-Village results would have a ready explanation in terms of the influence of external varieties of French on loss of the simple past, this seems less likely in the cases of both Saint-Louis and L'Anse-à-Canards. Recall that both the Saint-Louis and the L'Anse-à-Canards varieties were seen to be highly conservative with respect to pronoun choice and the morphology of the verb in the first- and third-person plural, shown in table 3.2, and with respect to preservation of the inflected future, with the relevant constraints remaining intact. What unites these two varieties (and Abram-Village as well) is dialect contact: in Prince

Edward Island such contact took place early on, with heterogeneous settlements established following the eighteenth-century return from exile and in Newfoundland, the same scenario resulted for one of its source dialects, that of Chéticamp, Nova Scotia. Likewise, heterogeneity of settlement characterizes the long-isolated Îles de la Madeleine, where Falkert (2005, 80) finds no evidence of either the simple past or the imperfect subjunctive. Newfoundland's Port-au-Port Peninsula saw additional, late-nineteenth-century dialect contact, involving new arrivals from Brittany and Normandy. While we know from Flikeid and Péronnet's (1989) late-twentieth-century survey that the nineteenth-century Chéticamp variety would have retained the simple past to some degree, we have no direct evidence for the late Metropolitan variety that provided a second, substantial set of francophone settlers to Newfoundland's west coast. We do know, though, that the simple past is almost entirely absent from the French data for the late-nineteenth-century *Atlas linguistique de la France* (Gilliéron and Édmont 1902–10). It may well be, then, that the simple past was lost from Newfoundland's west cost varieties due to dialect mixture.

As we might expect, the simple past is not attested in contemporary Cajun French, although we find scattered instances in performances of traditional folktales collected in 1923 in Avoyelles Parish and published by Saucier (1956). Conwell and Juilland (1963, 168) state that the simple past is not in use and also attest to a collapse of the distinction between the imperfect and present perfect, such that both express single, completed actions. This is what we would expect, given the situation of language shift that has resulted in the verbal paradigm presented in table 3.4.

## CONCLUSION

In this chapter, then, we have seen that particular varieties of Acadian French do present a kind of "window on the past" in that contrasts long argued to be lost or to be in the process of being lost are still made and that variant choice is constrained in ways reminiscent of the earlier history of the language attested by grammarians, historical linguists, and commentators (*remarqueurs*). We have also explored both the path of particular changes and the sociolinguistic settings that facilitate change, considering linguistic factors, such as saliency of particular forms, and social ones, such as dialect mixing and leveling.

# 4. THE EXPLOITATION
# OF VARIATION

As sociolinguists have clearly demonstrated, languages exhibit both stable variation and variation that is reflective of change in progress. A well-known case of stable variation in English is, of course, the (ing) variable: quantitative research conducted throughout the English-speaking world since the late 1950s has shown stylistically and socially based variation between velar and alveolar nasal variants. In French, one case of stable variation that has been the object of several studies is presence versus absence of the *que* 'that' complementizer, a phenomenon which has a long history in the language.[1] For instance, the data below (cited by Martineau 1988) are taken from twelfth- (example 1) and thirteenth-century (2) literary texts.

1. *Qui    que    s'en    aut,           sachiez        Ø    je    remendré.*
   who    that    REFL    go.3SG.SUBJ    know.2*pl.imper*    I    stay.1SG.FUT
   'Whoever goes, know I will stay' [*Aimeri de Narbonne*, v. 241]
2. *Je    cuit              pas    plus    sot    de    ti    Ø    n'    i*
   I    believe.SG.PRES    NEG    more    foolish    of    you        NEG    there
   *a*
   have.3SG.PRES
   'I believe there is no one more foolish than you' [*Jeu de la Feuillée*, v. 341]

Likewise, *que* absence is attested in the speech of the future king Louis XIII, recorded during his childhood and adolescence in the early seventeenth century by his personal physician, Jean Héroard (Ernst 1985). Such usage is illustrated in (3) and (4):[2]

3. *Je    panse              Ø    je    pisserai          dedans.*
   I    think.SG.PRES          I    piss-1SG.FUT    in
   'I think I will piss in it'
4. *La    sphaere    Ø    vous           m'avé           promise...*
   the    sphere          you    me.DAT    have-SG.IMP    promised
   'The sphere you promised me...'

Early-twentieth-century commentators like Bauche (1920) mention variable presence/absence of the complementizer and indeed such variation continues to be widespread in present-day French. The examples in (5) and (6) illustrate the variable with late-twentieth-century Saint-Louis, Prince Edward Island, data:

5. *Je       pense      qu'  ils   sont        gâtés     assez.*
   1PERS  think.SG.PRES  that  they  be.3PL.PRES  spoiled   enough
   'I think that they are pretty spoiled'

6. *Je       pense      Ø   j'   oublierai            jamais  ça.*
   1PERS  think.SG.PRES      1PERS  forget-1SG.FUT   never   that
   'I think I will never forget it'

I will not dwell here on how such usage is constrained phonologically and lexically, but refer the reader to the classic analysis of the variable in Montreal French by Sankoff (1980), as well as more recent Laurentian (Martineau 1988; Dion 2003) and Acadian (Beaulieu and Cichocki 2003; King and Nadasdi 2006) studies. We will return briefly to this variable in chapter 6 in the discussion of the expression of evidentiality in Acadian French.

I focus below on the kinds of paths grammatical variation may follow. First, I look at variation concerning lexical items that express the meaning 'at the house of' and how such variation is resolved, or not, in different varieties. Second, I consider change in the structure of yes/no questions in the history of French and how this change has played out in both Laurentian and Acadian varieties. Finally, I turn to a discussion of variation in third-person plural subject-verb agreement, presented in general terms in chapter 3. Here I consider this variable in one particular linguistic context, subject relative clauses, and trace the trajectory of change in agreement marking in a number of Acadian varieties.

## THE (ACADIAN) HISTORY OF FRENCH *CHEZ*

In the discussion of the expression of past temporal reference in French, I noted that grammarians often try to "make sense of" variation in the language: as demonstrated by Estienne's (1578) 24-hour rule, which attempts to capture the notion of temporal distance in the choice of simple past versus present perfect by stipulating that events taking place within 24 hours of the moment of speech be rendered with the latter and those taking place more than 24 hours prior to the moment of speech be rendered with the former. Another example of such a tendancy is Guillaume's well-known contrast (1929; cited by Blanche-Benveniste 1995, 129) between choice of mood in the embedded clause with *il est possible que* 'it is possible that', argued to trigger the subjunctive, and *il est probable que* 'it is probable that', argued to trigger the indicative.[3] What might be perceived as the preoccupations of grammarians are not, however, unlike the so-called naive speaker's attempts to sort out their language use. This would seem to be behind some fairly recent developments in a case of lexicogrammatical variation.

The present case involves native-speaker sorting out of variation with regard to the French equivalents of 'at the house of'. Acadian French inherited from Latin (by way of Old and Middle French) two ways of rendering this meaning: (1) *chus*, from Latin *casa* > Old French *chies* > Modern French *chez* (pronounced [ʃu] in Acadian French, as the dialect spelling indicates) and (2) *su* [sy], derived from either Latin *super* 'on, above' or Latin *sursum* 'at the top, toward the top'. *Casa* itself lost out early on to *maison* < *mansio* as the main way of expressing 'house' in French, though it survived into Old French in examples like *en chies son hoste* 'at his host's house' or *a ches nos* 'at our house' (Nyrop 1899–1930, 95; cited by Mougeon and Beniak 1991). Mougeon and Beniak (1991, 167) discuss the fact that bare *chies* > *chez* won out over fused forms *enchies* and *aches* in the history of the language.[4]

French *sur* < Latin *super* 'on, above' developed a *chez*-like meaning in the fourteenth or early fifteenth century (Wartburg 1966, 432; Littré 1968, 595; also cited by Mougeon and Beniak 1991), but died out in the standard language by the seventeenth century, though it survived dialectally. Yet another preposition, *sus* < Latin *sursum* 'at the top', is also attested at around the same time with this same meaning. While contemporary [sy] is a colloquial variant in both Laurentian and Acadian French, we cannot tell which Latin preposition it derives from due to historical tendencies toward final-consonant deletion, be it /s/ or /r/.

In Mougeon's 1970s Franco-Ontarian corpus, standard *chez* is in variation with vernacular *su*, and also with *à la maison de*, the latter a calque on English usage.[5] *Su* is attested, but infrequent, in their data. We turn now to usage in Acadian French varieties. First, recall that *chus* is the reflex of Old French *chies* in these varieties: native speaker consultants in Nova Scotia and Prince Edward Island whom I polled consider *chus* the vernacular variant and *chez* [ʃe] an "educated" variant, one they associate with out-group usage. While *chus* is in robust use in my Prince Edward Island corpora, *à la maison de* is in fact quite infrequent. Instead, *chus* and *su* are in complementary distribution in Abram-Village and Saint-Louis: *chus* typically selects a pronominal complement (e.g., *chus nous* 'at our house', *chus eux* 'at their house') while *su* selects a lexical complement (e.g., *su Philippe* 'at Philip's house', *su ma cousine* 'at my cousin's house'). In the Grosses Coques, Nova Scotia, corpus, *su* is also used with lexical complements, while *chus* is used with plural pronominal ones.[6] However, *su* is used for singular pronominal complements, rare in the Grosses Coques corpus. These comprise 2 of 167 usages of *su* with this meaning in the corpus. Philip Comeau (pers. comm., Apr. 1, 2012) points out that first-person plural *chus nous* would be used for the meaning of 'at my house' in Baie Sainte-Marie Acadian French, even if one were living alone. Examples (7)–(9) show that patterning of the two variants in the Grosses Coques corpus.

7. *Il  venait        droite  su              Robert.*
   he  come-SG.IMP  right   at.the.house.of  Robert
   'He came right to Robert's house'

8. *Il  l'  avait      dumpé    su             lui.*
   he  it  have-SG.IMP  dumped  at.the.house.of  him
   'He had dropped it off at his house'

9. *Elle  était      chus           eux    aujourd'hui.*
   she  be.SG.IMP  at.the.house.of  them  today
   'She was at their house today'

The few tokens with singular pronouns, such as (8), fall outside the general pattern and thus do not invalidate it.

When we look back in the historical record, Geddes's (1908) description of the Baie-Des-Chaleurs northeastern New Brunswick variety presents the same general distribution, though the data are presented without relevant commentary: a *chez* [ʃø] variant is found with strong pronouns and a *su* [sy] variant with lexical subjects. Geddes cites Jaubert (1864) for the central France origins of *su* usage. As for southeastern New Brunswick, the *Lettres à Marichette*, written by a native of the area, shows this same pattern. However, while both [ʃe] and [ʃø] pronunciations are attested for *chez* in the *Dictionary of Louisiana French* (2010), the extensive entry for *su(r)* does not include the meaning 'at the house of'. Likewise, I have never encountered the *su(r)* variant on Newfoundland's Port-au-Port peninsula, nor is it cited in Brasseur's *Dictionnaire des regionalismes du français de Terre-Neuve* (2001). However, *su(r)* (along with *chus*) is found in my interview corpus for neighboring Stephenville/Kippens, where only Acadians from the Maritime Provinces settled (i.e., there was no dialect mixture such as found on the peninsula). We may therefore assume that *su(r)* 'at the house of' was brought to Newfoundland by settlers from Chéticamp but may well have been absent from the variety spoken by its late-nineteenth-century Port-au-Port settlers whose origins were further north in France, in Brittany and Normandy. Leveling of variants would then have taken place on Port-au-Port peninsula but not in Stephenville/Kippens; it may be that such leveling also took place in French Louisiana.

There is a recent innovation with two prepositions in the Abram-Village, Prince Edward Island, corpus that involves the juxtaposition of standard *chez* [ʃe] with vernacular *su* [sy], as in (10):

10. *Ils     étiont       chez              su               Phillipe.*
    they be.3PL.IMP at.the.house.of at.the.house.of Philippe
    'They were at Philippe's house'

Although infrequent in the corpus, examples like (10) appear to involve hypercorrection, found only in that Prince Edward Island community most influenced by external varieties of French. The data come from speakers who rank high in terms of the sociolinguistic marketplace (Sankoff and Laberge 1978; following on Bourdieu and Boltonski 1975). Nevertheless, they represent one path by which supralocal usage may infiltrate the vernacular. Intuitively, *su(r)* seems to be fused with the lexical subject and *chez* the actual preposition, although the most obvious formal representation would have *chez* as a specifier and *su(r)* the actual head of the prepositional phrase. Keep in mind, though, that this is an innovative variant in the Abram-Village French grammar.

Interestingly, the incoming Ontario French variant, *à la maison de*, is unattested in the Grosses Coques and Newfoundland corpora and is quite rare in the Prince Edward Island corpora. So this case of variation seems largely unaffected by contact with English. In the next chapter, we will see that all Acadian varieties have borrowed a range of lexical (and I include some function words under this rubric) from English, but here we find "French" prepositional phrases, not English calques, to express the meaning 'at the house of'. What is most interesting for this variable is the "resolution" of variant competition through complementary distribution. This resolution may, of course, be undone, as in the case of the emerging Abram-Village variant, *chez su*.

## THE *TI* QUESTION MARKER IN FRENCH

Prescriptive grammars present the structure of yes/no questions in French in terms of subject-verb inversion, as in (11), with a lexical subject, and (12), with a pronominal subject.[7]

11. *Les garçons vont-      ils    partir    bientôt?*
    the boys      go.3PL.PRES they leave-INF soon
    'Are the boys going to leave soon?'
12. *Vont-       ils    partir    bientôt?*
    go.3PL.PRES they leave-INF soon
    'Are they going to leave soon?'

Both complex (example 11) and pronominal (example 12) inversion have existed in French since the Middle French (roughly 1300–1600) period (Foulet 1921).[8] Noninversion yes/no questions are also possible with the addition of *est-ce que* 'is it that', as in *Est-ce que les garçons vont partir bientôt?* Structures such as (11) are entirely absent from our Acadian sociolinguistic corpora (they are associated with formal French), while those like (12) have restricted distribution, as we shall see. What is interesting for the present discussion is that when the inverted verb ends in a vowel in the third person, an epenthetic *-t-* is inserted between the verb and the subject clitic, illustrated in (13):

13. *Va-     t-il   partir     bientôt?*
    go.3SG  he    leave-INF   soon
    'Is he going to leave soon?'

Epenthetic *-t-* in combination with the third-person singular masculine pronoun *il* was reanalyzed as a question particle, *ti*, as early as the seventeenth century in colloquial French (Harris 1978; Roberts 1993).[9] As Roberts points out, this reanalysis was dependent on the productivity of deletion of the final /l/ of the pronoun, which gave rise to the string /ti/. Roberts makes the case that the development of the *ti* question marker is associated with the loss of subject-clitic inversion in yes/no questions in colloquial French. Roberts also notes the existence of a *tu* variant of *ti* in varieties such as Quebec French, suggesting that the second-person singular clitic pronoun was the source of the question marker. With the development of the *ti* question marker, inversion is lost, as illustrated in (14):

14. *Il   va            ti   partir     bientôt?*
    he   go.3SG.PRES   Q   leave-INF   soon
    'Is he going to leave soon?'

In France, it would appear that the *ti* interrogative is in decline (Goosse 2000, 116; cited by Rowlett 2007, 207). However, this is not the case in contemporary Canadian varieties. In Laurentian varieties, the *tu* question particle is widespread (Elsig 2009).[10] Following Morin (1985), I would suggest that *tu* is a twentieth-century (Laurentian) development, involving further reanalysis—that is, *ti* gets interpreted as *tu*.[11]

In the Grosses Coques, Nova Scotia, variety, *ti* is used not only with third-person subjects, but with first-person subjects as well, as the data in (15)–(18) show:

15. *Je     te    l'   ai            ti   point  dit?*
    1PERS  you   it   have.1SG.PRES  Q   NEG    said
    'Didn't I tell you that?'

16. J'        avons           ti  parlé  de    ça    hier      à   la   club?
    1PERS have-1PL.PRES Q  talked about that yesterday at  the  club
    'Didn't we talk about that yesterday at the club?'

17. *Christine    a              ti vendu  sa    robe?*
    Christine have.3SG.PRES Q  sold   her  dress
    'Did Christine sell her dress?'

18. *Ils    venont           ti plus       te   visiter?*
    they come-3PL.PRES Q  any.more  us  visit-INF
    'Are they coming to see us any more?'

In the second-person singular and plural, there are no instances of either the *ti* or *tu* particle in the Grosses Coques corpus. Rather, we find rising intonation signaling the interrogative, as in (19), or pronominal inversion, as in (20) with the second-person singular and in (21) and (22), with the second-person plural (an option that appears limited in Acadian French to the second person):

19. *Tu      veux            point une  bière?*
    you.SG want.SG.PRES NEG   a    beer
    'Don't you want a beer?'

20. *Crois-             tu   dans des    ghosts?*
    believe.SG.PRES you  in   some  ghosts
    'Do you believe in ghosts?'

21. *Jean  dit,                "Voulez-   vous  boxer?"* [12]
    Jean  say.SG.PRES?SP?     want-2PL.PRES you  box-INF
    'Jean says/said, "Do you want to box"?'

22. *En   aviez-        vous   chus            vous?*
    some have-2PL.IMP you.PL at.the.house.of you.PL
    'Do you have any at home?'

We would thus want to argue that at some point *ti* spread from third person to first person in Grosses Coques Acadian, or in the earlier stage of the language from which the variety descends.[13] However, in the L'Anse-à-Canards, Newfoundland, variety, we find *ti* usage in the first and third person, along with a number of possibilities for the second person. First note that *vois-tu* 'do you see' is a frequently employed discourse marker in this variety, illustrated in (23):

23 *Il  restait         au    Cap Saint-Jean, vois-     tu,   puis il*
   he  stay-SG.IMP at.the Cap Saint-Jean see.SG.PRES you  and  he
   *rentrait             dans  L'Anse-à-Canards.*
   went.home-SG.IMP in    L'Anse-à-Canards
   'He was staying at Cap Saint-Jean, you see, and he went home to L'Anse-à-Canards'

Since discourse markers are fixed expressions, they do not illuminate the syntax of the present-day variety. However, the Butler Sociolinguistic Corpus contains a large number of L'Anse-à-Canards group interviews, which provide the conditions for both second-person singular and plural pronouns to occur. We find interrogation with *tu* and *vous* in the corpus expressed through rising intonation only, as in (24). Pronominal inversion is also found in folktale performance within the sociolinguistic interview, shown in (25).[14]

24. *Vous  vous  en  rappelez            du      Prieur?*
    you   REFL       remember.2PL.PRES  of.the  Prieur
    'You remember Prieur?'

25. *Joséphine,  dors-            tu,  là?*
    Joséphine   sleep.SG.PRES   you  there
    'Josephine, are you asleep?'

However, we also find *ti* interrogatives for both second-person singular and plural, as shown in (26) and (27):

26. *Tu  vas           ti  en  bas    à  la  côte?*
    you  go.SG.PRES   Q   in  down   at  the  coast
    'Are you going down to the shore?'

27. *Vous  avez            ti  assez   mangé?*
    you   have-2PL.PRES   Q   enough  eaten
    'Have you eaten enough?'

What can we make of variation between the two varieties? It would appear that in the Newfoundland variety the *ti* marker has spread from the third person throughout the paradigm (or rather, the corpus may preserve an earlier spread, keeping in mind we do not have access to early data for this variety or its source varieties). On the other hand, in Grosses Coques, the change appears to be "stuck": first and third person, but not second person, readily occur with *ti*.

The Prince Edward Island varieties appear to be at midpoint between the two cases, given that there only *ti* is found in the first and third persons, but *ti/tu* variation is found in the second-person singular.

28. *Ils  allont          ti  au      party  avec  nous-autres?*
    they  go-3PL.PRES    Q   to.the  party  with  us-others
    'Are they going to the party with us?'

29. *Tu  connais         tu  son  père?*
    you  know.SG.PRES   Q   his  father
    'Do you know his father?'

30. *Je     l'   avais         ti  laissé  au      club?*
    1PERS it  have-SG.IMP  Q  left    at.the  club
    'Had I left it at the club?'[15]

The Prince Edward Island varieties may actually mirror the early stages of a shift from *ti* to *tu*, which we know took place in Quebec French in the twentieth century.

Beaulieu (pers. comm., Apr. 2, 2008) reports *ti/tu* variation in her northeastern New Brunswick corpus for all three persons (although it should be noted that those few instances of *vous* in the corpus involve inversion, as in the Grosses Coques corpus). I exemplify this variation with data for the third-person singular and plural:[16]

31. *Ma  robe  est         ti  belle?*
    my  dress  be.3SG.PRES  Q  pretty
    'Is my dress pretty?'

32. *Elle  est          tu  âgée?*
    she  be.3SG.PRES  Q  elderly
    'Is she elderly?'

33. *Pis  les  enfants  fument            ti?*
    and  the  children  smoke.3PL.PRES  Q
    'And do the children smoke?'

34. *Tes  petites  amies    avaient        tu  des   idées  comme  ça?*
    your  little  friends  have.3PL.IMP  Q  some  ideas  like   that
    'Did your girlfriends have ideas like that?'

Some 100 years earlier, Geddes (1908, 119, 132) had recorded *ti* usage in the first and third person in the northeastern Baie-Des-Chaleurs variety but attests to only pronominal inversion for both the second-person singular and plural. It is highly likely, then, that Beaulieu's data reflects innovation since the time of Geddes' (late-nineteenth-century) fieldwork.

All of these Acadian varieties show yes/no question formation with the *ti* particle in at least part of the paradigm, with variable usage occurring in the second person in most cases. Not surprisingly, northeastern New Brunswick appears to be leaning toward the present-day Laurentian system in terms of use of the *tu* variant of the question marker. The Baie Sainte-Marie variety most likely preserves an earlier stage of the change, as it shows spread of *ti* from the third person to the first person: if *tu* were an innovative variant here, we might expect variation of the sort found in Prince Edward Island and present-day northeastern New Brunswick. The intercommunity variation with respect to this variable points to the necessity of describing these closely related varieties one at a time, rather than prematurely identifying an "Acadian" pattern. Interestingly, the *Dictionary of Louisiana French*

(2010, 614) gives attestations of the *ti* variant across the paradigm. I give one example from the dictionary with the second-person plural in (35):

35. *Vous avez       ti été     là-    bas?*
    you  have.2PL.PRES Q  been  there  below
    'Have you been over there?'

Table 4.1 presents the distribution of the *ti/tu* variants for several Acadian varieties and for present-day Quebec French. For several varieties, we have sketchy observations and/or data. Falkert (2005, 80) records *ti∼tu* variation in her Îles de la Madeleine corpus but notes the need for an in-depth study of variable usage. There is, however, very little commentary for southeastern New Brunswick in the linguistic literature, and, unfortunately, interrogatives of any sort are in short supply in the traditional folktale, as we have seen. They are also in short supply in the traditional one-on-one sociolinguistic interview, unless one includes the interviewer's speech.[17] However, artistic representations of the present-day southeastern variety look very much like the Quebec system: Dano LeBlanc's popular comic strip *Acadieman* shows a question particle as *tu* with first- and third-person pronouns and pronominal inversion in the second person. The data in (36) and (37) come from LeBlanc's (2009) collection of comic strips.

36. *Ej care- tu si les   Québécois   disent      'nuitte' pis 'litte'*
    I  care  Q  if the   Québécois   say.3PL.PRES 'nuitte' and 'litte'
    *oubédon    le   'parking'*
    or.well.then the  'parking'
    'Do I care if Québécois say 'nuitte' and 'litte' or even 'parking' (space)?'
37. *As-       tu  ever  wonderé   cousses  qué      l'   origine*
    have.SG.PRES you ever  wondered  what    that.it.is  the  origin
    *du    mot   chiac?*
    of.the word  chiac
    'Have you ever wondered what the origin of the word Chiac is?'

TABLE 4.1
Distribution of *tu/ti* Variants in Several North American Varieties

|  |  | *La.* | *NL* | *P.E.I.* | *N.S.* | *NNB₁* | *NNB₂* | *Queb.* |
|---|---|---|---|---|---|---|---|---|
| 3rd person | singular | *ti* | *ti* | *ti* | *ti* | *ti* | *ti∼tu* | *tu* |
|  | plural | *ti* | *ti* | *ti* | *ti* | *ti* | *ti∼tu* | *tu* |
| 1st person | singular | *ti* | *ti* | *ti* | *ti* | *ti* | *ti∼tu* | *tu* |
|  | plural | *ti* | *ti* | *ti* | *ti* | *ti* | *ti∼tu* | *tu* |
| 2nd person | singular | *ti* | *ti* | *ti∼tu* | — | — | *ti∼tu* | *tu* |
|  | plural | *ti* | *ti* | *ti∼tu* | — | — | *ti∼tu* | *tu* |

NNB₁ = Geddes 1908; NNB₂ = Beaulieu 1994.

Since the 1960s, there is much contact between urban Moncton (home, for example, to a francophone university) and Quebec; we might, therefore, expect that the *tu* variant of the question marker has also spread in nonartistic contexts of language use.

## SUBJECT VERB AGREEMENT IN SUBJECT RELATIVE CLAUSES

In their discussions of working-class European French, early-twentieth-century commentators Henri Frei (1929) and Henri Bauche (1920/1946) give examples of what I will refer to as default singulars in subject relative clauses. Example (38) is from Frei, and example (39) is from Bauche. Although the head of the relative is plural, the embedded verb is in the singular.

38. *J' aime       pas les femmes   qui    boit.*
    I  like.SG.PRES NEG the women who   drink.SG.PRES
    'I don't like women who drink'

39. *les hommes qu'  a                 vendu la    France...*
    the men      who  have.3SG.PRES sold   the   France
    'the men who sold France...'

The actual status of default singulars is not made clear in these works, though we might assume their use to be sporadic. Such is also the case for present-day Ontario French, where Mougeon and Beniak (1991) have linked certain types of nonagreement, such as that found in (40), with a main clause lexical subject, to English dominance. These researchers found that French-dominant speakers' use of default singulars appears to be limited to subject relatives, as in (41)—data reminiscent of those presented by Bauche and Frei. Such usage was fairly infrequent in Mougeon and Beniak's data.

40. *Les singes   peut        faire   qu'  est-ce qu'  on   peut*
    the monkeys can.SG.PRES do-INF what it is   that one can.SG.PRES
    *faire.*
    do-INF
    'Monkeys can do what we can do'

41. *Y    a             beaucoup de    choses qui   s'     produit.*
    there have.SG.PRES a lot       PART things that REFL go.on.SG.PRES
    'There are a lot of things going on'

In Laurentian and European spoken French varieties, as in Standard French, the third-person singular and plural are homophonous except when the verb is in the inflected future (e.g., *il aura* 'he will have' ~ *ils auront* 'they will have') or in that small number of cases in which there is alternation in the shape of the stem, with irregular verbs (e.g., *il peut* 'he can' ~ *ils peuvent* 'they can').[18] Orthographic *-ent*, then, is phonetically null except in liaison contexts, such as with pronominal inversion (e.g., *Mangent-ils du pain?* 'Are they eating bread?', where final /t/ would be pronounced). Here we will consider the patterning of variation in the L'Anse-à-Canards variety. Examples (42) and (43) below give examples of Acadian *-ont* taken from the L'Anse-à-Canards corpus. The third-person singular forms common to all varieties and the corresponding Standard French plurals are also indicated.

42. *Les gens    de    delà,    ils    parlont    curieux.*
    the people from there they speak-3PL.PRES funny
    'The people from there, they speak funny'
    [3rd-person sing.: *il parle*; SF 3rd-person plural: *ils parlent*]

43. *Ils    voyiont    une lumière à    tous    les    soirs.*
    they see-3PL.IMP a light at all the evenings
    'They used to see a light every evening'
    [3rd-person sing.: *il voyait*; SF 3rd-person plural: *ils voyaient*]

As we saw in chapter 3, the L'Anse-à-Canards speakers stand out as extremely conservative in their use of both first- and third-person verbal morphology. Indeed, the three "non-Acadian" tokens found in the entire L'Anse-à-Canards corpus were two instances of *vont* (vs Acadian *allont*) and one of *font* (vs Acadian *faisont*).[19] Thus, when plurality was marked on the verb, *-ont* is always used; what varied in these three cases was whether the Acadian stem was used or not.

In their 1989 study of New Brunswick and Nova Scotia varieties, Flikeid and Péronnet found one clear case of statistically significant intercommunity variation with regard to agreement marking on the verb. Île-Madame and, to a lesser extent, Pomquet, diverge from other Nova Scotia Acadian communities and from southeastern New Brunswick with respect to number marking in relative clauses, as shown in table 4.2. What Flikeid and Péronnet found in this context was a far greater preponderance of default singular usage in one of the varieties, that of Île-Madame, and a greater preponderance of the Acadian third-person plural usage (i.e., the *-ont* suffix) in the other varieties, with the exception of Pomquet, which falls in an intermediary position. While Flikeid and Péronnet do not specify whether or not object relatives are involved, all of their examples consist of subject relatives. Examples (43) (from Baie Sainte-Marie) and (44) (from Île-Madame) are taken from their study.

TABLE 4.2

Comparison of Use of the Traditional Third-Person Plural
by Clause Type for Several Acadian Varieties
(Flikeid and Péronnet 1989)

| Region | Average Proportion Acadian Usage | |
| --- | --- | --- |
| | *Relative Clauses* | *Other Contexts* |
| Pubnico, N.S. | .70 | .73 |
| Chéticamp, N.S. | .76 | .84 |
| Baie Ste-Marie, N.S. | .70 | .72 |
| Ile Madame, N.S. | .01 | .78 |
| Pomquet, N.S. | .61 | .87 |
| Southeast, N.B. | .64 | .70 |

43. ... *des   Anglaises        qui   veniont          pis   il   changiont*
        some  English.women  who  come-3PL.IMP  and  they  change-3PL.IMP
    *de   classe*
    of   class
    '...English women who came and they changed class'

44. ... *avec   des   grandes   familles   qui   vient            alentour   des*
        with  some  big      families  who  come.SG.PRES  around   some
    *maisons,   là*
    houses    there
    '...with big families who come around the houses'

Example (43) shows third-person plural *veniont* while example (44)
shows the default singular, *vient*. Since the relative clause data were not part
of their principal analysis, Flikeid and Péronnet do not attempt an explanation of these specific findings for Île-Madame and Pomquet. However,
in their general discussion of intercommunity differences, they note a less
firmly entrenched tradition of French education and less contact with other
francophones in these two communities than in the other communities
under study. Table 4.3 gives a parallel breakdown of data extracted from

TABLE 4.3

Comparison of Use of the Traditional Third-Person Plural
by Clause Type, L'Anse-à-Canards
(King 1994, 2005)

| Clause Type | Plural Marking | Singular Marking | Ambiguous Data |
| --- | --- | --- | --- |
| Subject Relatives | 8 | 30 | 27 |
| All Other Clause Types | 423 | 1 | 12 |
| Total *N*s | 431 | 31 | 39 |

interviews for 8 older speakers (4 male and 4 female) from the L'Anse-à-Canards subcorpus—a sample matching those studied in the Flikeid and Péronnet study. These interviews provided some 501 tokens in total. Examples of clear singular marking are given in (45) and (46):

> 45. *Il    y    a           ti    d'    autres histoires qui    vous*
>     it   there have.SG.PRES Q   some  other  stories  that  you.DAT
>     *vient          dans  l'    idée?*
>     come.SG.PRES   in    the   idea
>     'Are there other stories that come to mind?'
>
> 46. *Il    y    a            en   masse de   choses   qu'   a*
>     it   there have.SG.PRES in   lot   of   things   that  have.SG.PRES
>     *arrivé?*[20]
>     happened
>     'Are there a lot of things that have happened?'

While the results in table 4.3 show a striking difference between subject relatives and other clause types with respect to number marking on the verb, they also show that there are a number of ambiguous tokens. Tokens were classed as ambiguous if they were homophonous with the regular standard or colloquial French plural usage. Examples are given in (47)–(49).

> 47. *Il    y    a             un   car  devant       nous-autres, un   gros  Chev,*
>     it   there have.SG.PRES  a    car  in.front.of  us-others    a    big   chev
>     *tu    sais,  puis  deux  vieilles femmes   qui    [drayve].*
>     you   know   and   two   old      women    who    drive.3SG?3PL?.IMP
>     'There's a car in front of us, a big Chev, you know, and two old women who
>     were driving'
>
> 48. *Toujours,  le    Hood  avait         été    coulé,   hein,  comme  ça,*
>     anyway     the   Hood  have.SG.IMP   been   flooded  eh     like   that
>     *tous  ceux   qu'   étiont,          qu'   [ete]   à              bord*
>     all    those  that  be.3SG?3PL?.IMP  on    board   have.3PL.PRES
>     *ont   été    noyé.*
>     been   drowned.
>     'Anyway, the Hood [name of boat] was flooded, eh, like that, all that were,
>     that were on board were drowned'
>
> 49. *Il    y    a            des    choses  qui    fait          peur,  puis*
>     it   there have.SG.PRES some   things  which  make.SG.PRES  fear   and
>     *d'    autres  qu'   est,           qui    [dɔn]          la    joie.*
>     some  others  which be.3SG.PRES    which  give.SG?PL?.PRES the   joy
>     'There are things that make you afraid and there are others that are, that
>     give you joy'

However, I argue that these potentially ambiguous cases are best analyzed as default singulars. The results presented in table 4.3 show that, in all other contexts, Acadian *-ont* occurs in the vast majority of cases; indeed, there are no unambigous *-ent* forms (such as *peuvent* 'are able to' or *savent* 'know', which involve plural stems). In theory, [drayve] in (47) could be *drivait* or *drivaient*. However, *drivaient* would seem unlikely, since if the verb were in the plural, the expected ending would be the nonstandard imperfect *-iont* rather than the standard *-aient*, given that the plural form always has *-ont*. An examination of some other ambiguous sentences also points toward this analysis. Example (48) shows self-correction on the part of the informant, who has no unambiguously Standard French usage, so it seems most likely that the form [ete] is singular *était*, rather than plural *étaient*. Example (49) shows the verb *donne* (homophonous with Standard French *donnent*), but it is contained within a string of unequivocal default singulars. Thus, both the overall quantitative results and the analysis of particular examples support reclassification of the ambiguous cases as default singulars.

The data were coded for grammatical distinctions that might affect agreement, including clause type, verb type (auxiliary, modal, or lexical verb), and tense/aspect distinctions, some of which were suggested by earlier studies of agreement in French varieties (e.g., by Mougeon and Beniak 1991). The data were also coded for speaker sex.

Some constructions occurred only rarely.[21] For example, there were only two instances of compound subjects (both with default singular verb forms) and only three *it*-clefts (all three containing default singular verb forms). Compound subjects were removed from the quantitative analysis, while *it*-clefts were included under subject relatives.[22] Table 4.4 gives a breakdown of the results of multivariate analysis obtained through the use of the Goldvarb statistical program. These results confirm that it is the subject relative construction that is at issue. Plural marking occurs in only

TABLE 4.4

Effects of Potential Conditioning Factors on Third-Person Plural
Subject-Verb Agreement for L'Anse-à-Canards
(King 1994, 2005b)

| *Factor Groups* | *Factor Weights* | *N* | |
|---|---|---|---|
| Clause Type | | | |
| Subject relatives | .01 | 8/65 | (12%) |
| Other clause types | .67 | 423/436 | (97%) |
| Range | 66 | | |

NOTE: Factor groups not selected: verb type, verb tense, speaker sex.

12% of tokens in this environment but in 97% of tokens in all other environments. (I return to that small number of cases where plural agreement is actually made in subject relatives below.) The examples below for object relatives show that it is subject relatives, not relative clauses in general, that are relevant. As (50) and (51) show, in object relatives the verb agrees in number with a plural antecedent, as indicated by the presence of the *-ont* suffix.

50. *Il y      a           une gigue asteure qu' ils     jouont.*
    it there have.SG.PRES a    jig    now    that they play-3PL.PRES
    'Now, there's a jig that they play'

51. *...des    maladies   que les bêtes             avont        ou*
    some sicknesses that the farm.animals have-3PL.PRES or
    *de quoi     comme ça.*
    something like    that
    '...sicknesses that (farm) animals have or something like that'

How are we to explain the pattern shown in tables 4.3 and 4.4? Agreement in Standard French relative clauses works as it does in Standard English in that agreement ultimately holds between the verb and the head of the relative:

52. *la fille qui va         à l'  école...*
    the girl who go.3SG.PRES to the school
    'the girl who goes to school...'

53. *les filles qui vont       à l'  école...*
    the girls who go.3PL.PRES to the school
    'the girls who go to school...'

In Standard English and French, the head of the relative and the verb contained within the relative must share the same number marking. This agreement in features is mediated by a coindexing relation between *who* (or *qui*) and the head of the relative—from a Minimalist perspective (Chomsky 1992, 2001), subject to feature checking and valuation under Agree. However, the Newfoundland equivalent, shown in (54), is not so straightforward.

54. *les filles qui va         à l'  école...*
    the girls who go.3SG.PRES to the school
    'the girls who go to school...'

But while number is not transmitted to the verb in this construction, another feature associated with the nominal domain, gender, is in fact transmitted, since in the example in (55) the head of the relative *les affaires* and the predicate adjective *curieuse* [tʃɔrijøz] (compare the masculine *curieux* [tʃɔrijø]) are both feminine. Any analysis of the data, then, must account for the transmission of gender but not number.

55. *les affaires qu' a été curieuse...*
    the things that have.3SG.PRES been strange
    'things that were strange...'

There are also some instances of third-person plural agreement marking in subject relatives, in contradiction to the generalization, which need to be accounted for. While one must expect some amount of data fluctuation, it is noteworthy that all of these instances of third-person plural agreement have what appears at first glance to be just the clitic *en* as the head; that is, they involve *il y en a* 'there are some' or *il y en avait* 'there were some'. There is evidence that *il y en a* is a frozen expression in this variety and in a number of other varieties of colloquial French. Nadasdi (2000), for instance, makes such a case for Ontario French, pointing out that it is only in this expression that the clitic pronouns *y* and *en* actually co-occur in this variety. The same distribution is found in Acadian French. However, close inspection of the data shows a clear contrast between examples such as (56) with bare *il y en a* and those such as (57) with *il y en a dix-huit* 'there are eighteen of them' and (58) with *il y a deux hommes* 'there are two men'.[23] The contrast centers on whether or not there is an identifiable head of the relative. Specifically, the relatives in (57) and (58) have identifiable heads while the one in (56) is essentially headless.

56. *Des fois il y en a qui s' assisont*
    some times it there some have.3SG.PRES who REFL sit-3PL.PRES
    *sur les jambes...*
    on the legs
    'Sometimes there are some who sit on their legs...'

57. *Il y en a dix-huit qu' a été*
    it there some have.SG.PRES eighteen who have.3SG.PRES been
    *tué.*
    killed
    'There were eighteen of them that were killed'

58. *Il y a deux hommes qu' a venu à*
    it there have.SG.PRES two men who have.3SG.PRES come to
    *la porte.*
    the door
    'There were two men who came to the door'

To summarize, then, the agreement facts to be accounted for are as follows:

A. in all clause types except subject relatives, overt plural agreement appears to be categorical (e.g., *les filles partont* 'the girls are leaving');

B. subject relatives have default singular marking (e.g., *je connais les filles qui partit*), but overt gender marking is found (e.g., *les filles qu' était heureuse* 'the girls that were happy');[24]

C. the *il y en a* subtype of subject relatives in which *il y en a* has an overt head (e.g., *il y en a deux…* 'there are two of them') triggers default singular marking, but bare *il y en a* has overt plural marking on the verb.

I begin with the status of relative *qui* (versus interrogative *qui*). In French generally, interrogative *qui* is never used with inanimates, but no such distinction exists for relative *qui* (see, e.g., [10] and [40]).[25] There is a long tradition in French syntax, dating from Kayne (1974), to consider relative *qui* as a variant of the *que* complementizer, more recently as the realization of *que* + agr(eement) (Rizzi 1990), thus entailing a dependency between T(ense) and C(omplemetizer). As for the syntactic structure of the relative clause itself, the relative clause (a CP) is adjoined to the NP, as in (59), *les filles qui partit* 'the girls who is [*sic*] leaving':

59. $_{DP}$[les $_{NP}$[ $_{NP}$[filles] $_{CP}$[qui partit]]]

There has been considerable debate dating from the 1980s on as to whether the head of relative clauses is base generated outside of CP and linked to a null operator (OP) in CP by a predication relation or whether the head raises to SpecCP. Since neither approach appears to have implications for the present analysis, I adopt the former, as exemplified in (60), where, for clarity of exposition, I have inserted the overt morphology of the complementizer and the verb:

60. $_{DP}$[les $_{NP}$[ $_{NP}$[filles]] $_{CP}$[OP$_i$ qui$_j$ $_{TP}$[t$_i$ t$_i$ partit$_k$ $_{VP}$[t$_i$ t$_k$]]]]

The patterns found in (A)–(C) above involve variable number marking on the verb depending on the construction type. I assume, following both later Minimalism (Chomsky 2001) as well as the theory of Distributed Morphology (Halle and Marantz 1993), that a linguistic item is a bundle of morphological features.[26] In this view, inflectional elements are inserted on the verb in the phonological component, following the syntax. Thus, in the analysis that follows, it is the abstract features for person, gender, and number that are checked and valued in the syntax, not the overt morphology.

Under Minimalism, person, gender, and number, the relevant features for the current analysis, are interpretable (by the semantics) on the DP (e.g., *les filles* 'the girls' designates a set of individuals) but not on the verb (e.g., there is no plurality of events in *les filles partont* 'the girls are leaving'). Uninterpretable features must be checked and valued through the operation Agree: for instance, the Tense head must be paired with the plural feature on the subject DP, thus associating plurality with Tense; Tense itself must be paired with the verb, thus associating plurality with the verb (see figure 4.1). (Note that Tense and the subject DP also agree for nominative case.)[27] Subsequently, the DP subject moves to the specifier position of TP and the verb raises to T. Once the phase is complete, the derivation undergoes Spell-Out and is submitted to the phonological and semantic components. The checked features are accessible to the phonological component and it is here that overt agreement marking (in this case the third-person plural *-ont* suffix) is inserted on the verb. The L'Anse-à-Canards data also show overt gender agreement with predicate adjectives. Gender morphology is likewise inserted in the phonological component (e.g., *les filles sont heureuse* 'the girls are happy').

As for the patterns found in (B) and (C), the discussion of subject relatives and the status of the *qui* (< *que*) complementizer leads us to assume

FIGURE 4.1
Structure of a Simple Transitive Clause

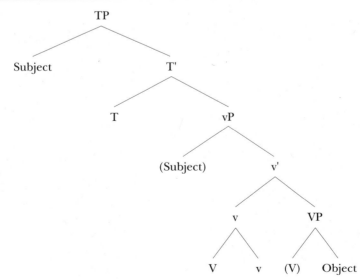

multiple Agree relations in the derivation of these structures. Recall that
Rizzi (1990) has argued that relative *qui* is the overt realization of *que* +
agr(eement): it would follow logically that agr in C is co-indexed with agr
in T. Further, Pesetsky and Torrego (2001, n. 73) suggest that, like English
*that*, French *qui* is an instance of T moved to C.[28] I assume, then, that subject relatives have the structure in figure 4.2. Feature checking involves: (1)
for Tense, checking both *u*Case and *u*Phi (person, gender, and number)
features against OP; (2) for the null operator, checking *u*Case against Tense
and checking *u*Rel against C (under the assumption that C has an interpretable Rel feature); and (3) for the complementizer, checking *u*Tense
via T-to-C movement (Tense bears Phi-features from *que* + agr = *qui*), and
checking *u*OP against the null operator.

   While I have accounted for all of the relevant uninterpretable features
in the structure, I have not addressed the issue of how it is that plural morphology is sometimes overt, sometimes not. The basic pattern is that when
there is an overt "antecedent" and when there is also a predication relationship such as exists between an NP and a relative clause, plural is not
overtly marked but rather there is default singular marking. Since number marking is variable in this way, some of the phonological features of a
lexical item must be available from the beginning of the derivation: that is,
the head of the relative must carry some phonological features or it would
not otherwise be possible for the phonological component to "decide" that

FIGURE 4.2
Structure of French Subject Relatives

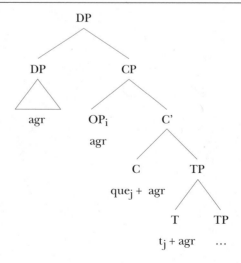

agreement morphology should not be spelled out on the verb. Within the theory of Distributed Morphology, it is not possible to change the feature specification of a lexical item, but it is possible to insert underspecified (default) morphemes.[29] In the presence of a phonologically visible head, then, default singular marking is inserted in the phonological component.

This is the case with subject relatives of the non–*il y en a* type, where we do not get overt plural agreement with an antecedent but rather default number marking. While the plural feature is not spelled out, the adjective does overtly agree in gender with the head of the subject relative clause, as in (61):

61. $_{DP}$[les $_{NP}$[ $_{NP}$[filles]] $_{CP}$[OP$_i$ qui$_j$ $_{TP}$[t$_i$ t$_j$ a éték $_{VP}$[t$_i$ t$_k$ $_{SP}$[t$_i$ curieuse]]]]]

Likewise, in *il y en a* relatives with an identifiable head, there is no insertion of the *-ont* suffix, but rather the verb always occurs in the default singular form. In contrast, with bare *il y en a*, there is variation in individual speakers' usage. For some speakers, constructions with *il y en a* pattern like other subject relatives; for others, there is overt plural marking. What would account for plural marking with bare *il y en a*? The most likely explanation is that overt plural marking on the verb in what is a headless construction for these speakers is a strategy to spell out the number of the subject in the absence of an overt head bearing this feature.

While most studies of subject-verb agreement in French do not go into the degree of detail presented above, there is clear evidence of some degree of variation in other varieties along the lines I have suggested here. In a study of third-person plural marking in Prince Edward Island French, King and Nadasdi (1996) found a contrast between speakers who were resident of Abram-Village and residents of Saint-Louis, the latter the community with least contact with other varieties of French. The Prince Edward Island case presents a more complex picture than did the Newfoundland one, due first to a wider array of variants, including, along with clearly normative French usage as well as vernacular usage, a much higher proportion of ambiguous cases. Therefore, a larger sample size was used for this particular study, involving 5,000 tokens for 26 speakers, representative of the two communities, both sexes, and a wide age range. The overall results according to community are presented in table 4.5. That community emerged as significant in multivariate analysis of the potential effects of a number of linguistic and social variables is explicable in terms of the differing social circumstances of French in the two communities.[30] With regard to linguistic constraints on variation, however, the clause-type constraint that approaches categoriality in Newfoundland did exert some effect on variation, but, while subject

TABLE 4.5
Proportion of Use of the Traditional Third-Person Plural Suffix -ont
by Prince Edward Island Community.

| | |
|---|---|
| Saint-Louis | 1,432/1,733 (83%) |
| Abram-Village | 2,105/3,109 (68%) |

relative clauses disfavor overt plural marking on the verb, the effect was fairly weak.

Another conditioning effect emerged in this study, not uncovered in previous studies of the variable: the effect of subject type. Note that in King and Nadasdi's investigation of linguistic constraints on subject-verb agreement, a somewhat different partitioning of third-person plural variation was used in this study in that the data were analyzed along a singular versus plural dimension (i.e., all overt manifestations of plurality, not uniquely vernacular usage, are contrasted with cases of overt singular marking). With the pronominal subject *ils*, plural marking was more likely to occur than with a lexical subject, 79% versus 71%, respectively, which was found to be statistically significant in multivariate analysis. Subsequent studies of another Acadian variety (Beaulieu and Cichocki 2003 for northeastern New Brunswick Acadian) and of Louisiana Cajun French (Dubois, King, and Nadasdi 2004) also found evidence of such an effect.[31] Intuitively, these results seem related to the fact that *ils* is not overtly marked for number, being homophonous with third-person masculine singular *il* 'he'. Thus, when there is a subject pronoun, number cannot be recovered from the subject, similar to the bare *il y en a* case noted above for the Newfoundland variety. But more would appear to be at issue since, crosslinguistically, pronouns are more likely to trigger agreement than are other types of subjects (Henry 2002, 277). It may be, then, that variation linked to subject type in these Acadian varieties falls out from universal tendencies.

If there is only a slight tendency toward default singulars in subject relatives in these other varieties of French, one might ask how two varieties of Acadian French became so "advanced," those of Île-Madame, Nova Scotia (see Flikeid and Péronnet 1989), and L'Anse-à-Canards, Newfoundland. The fact that several Acadian varieties behave no differently from other colloquial varieties of French points to New World and most likely post-deportation innovation in these two communities. Following their return from exile in the mid- to late 1700s, the Acadian people formed small, isolated communities, some of which underwent fairly rapid assimilation to English, while others remained francophone enclaves. In Newfoundland, settlement was fairly late, with the first Acadian settlers of western

Newfoundland arriving from Chéticamp, Nova Scotia, near the end of the eighteenth century, as we saw in chapter 2. There has been no contact of which I am aware between the Newfoundland settlers and the residents of Île-Madame. As shown in table 4.2, the separation of subject relative from all other clause types does not occur in the French of Chéticamp, while the distinction is clearcut in the Newfoundland variety and in the French of Île-Madame. While Chéticamp speakers exhibit weak tendencies toward the agreement pattern discussed here, the oldest French Newfoundlanders I recorded (people born at the turn of the twentieth century) have near-categorial use of default singulars in subject relatives. This would then point to an independent development whereby a tendency toward a default singular has become a fully fledged feature of the grammar. The two Acadian varieties with default singular usage as the norm have a common sociolinguistic feature: historically there has been very low, indeed almost nonexistent, normative pressure in the direction of Standard French. This would also appear to be the case for Cajun French, where Dubois, King, and Nadasdi (2004) have shown that, while the traditional variant is much less frequent than in the Acadian varieties discussed above, in subject relative clauses default singulars are categorical. The Louisiana setting is one setting in which rapid change in the direction described here could occur.

However, it is not the case that such change necessarily occurs in such a setting, as evidenced by the Saint-Louis, Prince Edward Island, facts, where clause type exhibits a weak effect on variation. This result is somewhat surprising, given that Saint-Louis residents have stood out as heavy vernacular users in a number of studies of other variables, such as *je… ons* retention (King, Nadasdi, and Butler 2004). Thus, a situation of very low normative pressure may provide a setting in which the default singular pattern may take hold, but it is not necessarily the case that this will actually happen. In other words, it may provide a necessary but not a sufficient condition for change.

## CONCLUSION

In this chapter I have examined a number of cases of intercommunity variation: variation in ways of rendering 'at the house of', variation in choice of Q marker (*tu* vs. *ti*) and its spread from the third person to other persons, and variation in third-person plural agreement marking. I have appealed to data from a variety of sources and to quantitative methodology and, in the final case, to formal theory, for an understanding of finely grained linguistic variation and its outcomes.

# 5. TRAJECTORIES OF CHANGE

IN THIS CHAPTER, I present variable data involving small sets of lexical items, for which I consider possible trajectories of variation and change. The role of lexical diffusion is not particularly controversial in work on grammatical change (see, e.g., Harris and Campbell 1995); what the present work offers is close attention to the process. I first present a case that, at first glance, appears to present evidence for (New World) innovation with respect to auxiliary selection but on close inspection of the historical record shows itself to be more complex. In the second example, I consider the set of prepositions across Acadian varieties which allow preposition stranding, that is, fronting of the complement of the preposition but not the preposition itself. For example, all Acadian varieties allow the stranding of *pour* (e.g., *Qui as-tu voté pour?* 'Who did you vote for?'), but only the most "advanced" allow the stranding of *à* (e.g., *Qui as-tu parlé à?* 'Who did you speak to?'). This second case turns out to be lexical diffusion against the backdrop of contact-induced change.

## AUXILIARY SELECTION IN FRENCH

Auxiliary selection in Standard French is often the bane of second-language learners and of native speakers as well: a particular set of intransitive verbs are conjugated with *être* in the compound tenses: *être* selection includes a small number of verbs involving inherently directed motion (such as *arriver* 'to arrive' and *sortir* 'to leave') and a small number of verbs involving a change of state (such as *naître* 'to be born' and *s' habiller* 'to get dressed'). All pronominal verbs are conjugated with *être* (e.g., *se marier* 'to get married', *s'en aller* 'to go off', etc.), and, of course, *être* is the passive auxiliary. The familiar unergative/transitive (*habere* 'have') and unaccusative (*esse* 'be') split would have been in place by Late Latin/Early Romance (Ledgeway 2011, 455).[1] While we will not delve very deeply into the theoretical literature here, note that from a formal perspective auxiliary selection is argued to be triggered by the selectional properties of functional heads, little *v* in the case of change of state, motion, and the like verbs (Roberts 2007, 300–305, in an update of Burzio 1986) and the *se* pronoun in the case of pronominal verbs (Reinhart and Siloni 2005).

In colloquial French, contemporary researchers on both sides of the Atlantic have recorded variation in auxiliary selection with unaccusatives. Esch (2002) studied the diaries and letters of a resident of Nancy, a city in northeastern France, for the period 1916–91. Esch shows that while *avoir* was the main auxiliary used during the speaker's youth, and thus, we may assume, the local vernacular variant, he adopted the system taught in the educational system in later life. Jones (2001) presents evidence of variable auxiliary selection in the traditional Norman French variety spoken on Jersey in the Channel Islands: for instance, *venir* 'to come' and *aller* 'to go' are conjugated with *avoir*, not *être*, while *entrer* 'to enter' and *arriver* 'to show' show variable usage, albeit in a relatively small corpus.

Auxiliary variation existed from very early on in the history of French and indeed Romance in general.[2] In the authoritative *Le bon usage*, Grevisse (1986, §656) notes that in Old French bare forms like *j'ai levé* 'I got up' (along with pronominal forms *je me suis levé* and *je m'ai levé*) were certainly possible. While *être* ultimately won out in the literary language (e.g., *je me suis levé*), auxiliary variation has survived colloquial French as Grevisse notes with regard to *la langue populaire*). The claim that such variation has survived in colloquial French is echoed by Wagner and Pichon (1991). Further, it is noteworthy that the sixteenth-century grammarian Gilles de Guez (cited by Hatcher 1942, 141; in turn cited by Giancarli 2011, 210) reminds his readers that *être* is the correct auxiliary for pronominal verbs, strongly suggesting that *avoir* was (still) being used in just that context. Studies of Classical (seventeenth-century) French show clear variation with respect to auxiliary selection for (more than 30) intransitive verbs, despite the fact that grammarians and other commentators of the period actively proscribed *avoir*.[3] For instance, late-seventeenth-century commentators Vaugelas (1690) and Andry de Boisregard (1689) condemned usage such as *il a entré* 'he entered', *il a descendu* 'he came down', and *il a monté* 'he went up'. Such proscription suggests that not only lower-class speakers, but also higher-class speakers, must have exhibited variable usage in this regard since consumers of prescriptive grammars would be those high enough on the social ladder that upward mobility would have been possible. There would be no need to condemn usage already relegated to lower-class speech.

Fournier's (1998) survey of Classical French documents variable auxiliary selection for intransitives but makes no mention of pronominal verbs, in keeping with Nyrop's (1899–1930, 215) assertion that, after the Middle Ages, this particular use of *avoir* disappeared from the written, literary language. Similarly, Tailleur's (2007) quantitative analysis of auxiliary selection in seventeenth-century literary texts makes no mention of pronominal verbs. Tailleur found that intransitive verbs involving change of location (e.g., *monter* 'to go up'), change of state (e.g., *apparaître* 'to appear'), and continuation of a preexisting state (e.g., *rester* 'to stay') pattern together, exhibiting (similar) variable usage. These findings provide support for

Sorace's (2000) proposal of a cross-linguistic auxiliary selection hierarchy, as verbs which would fall lower on the hierarchy are found only with *avoir*.

The *Atlas linguistique de la France* (Gilliéron and Édmont 1902–10) includes maps of data from the turn of the twentieth century for both intransitive (e.g., (…) *est tombé* '…fell' [map 1312]) and pronominal verbs (*je me suis assis* 'I sat down' [map 500]). *Avoir* is widely used in the north with intransitive verbs and, with some exceptions, with pronominal verbs. In the province of Poitou, a major source of Acadian emigration to the New World, we see mostly *avoir* with pronominal verbs. This pattern is confirmed by map 508 (*vous vous êtes blessé* 'you injured yourself') and by mid-twentieth-century grammars and glossaries for the Vendée (Svenson 1959; Rézeau 1976; Gachignard 1983) and Deux-Sèvres (Pelmont 1994) varieties in the province of Poitou, varieties which are now at best moribund, if not entirely vanished.[4] Finally, in the early twentieth century, Frei (1929, 208–9) would refer to *avoir* usage with pronominal verbs as part of *le français avancé*; recall that Frei's work was based (at least in part) on analysis of a corpus of letters written by World War I French prisoners of war.

Crossing the Atlantic, we find that variable auxiliary selection is mentioned in the earliest dialect description of both Laurentian and Acadian French. Geddes (1908, 161) presents a short section on pronominal verbs in his description of the Carleton, New Brunswick, variety, concluding that "[pronominal] verbs are invariably conjugated with *avoir*." Interestingly, he cites Legendre (1890, 56), who remarks that such usage is quite rare in "Canadian" (i.e., Laurentian) French. Moving forward in time, in the LeBlanc folktale text from southeastern New Brunswick presented by Haden (1948), we find just such usage (also present in the folktale collected by Massignon 1947 in Baie Sainte-Marie, Nova Scotia, from the same period):[5]

1 *Elle  s'       a                  mis  à    brailler.*
  she  REFL  have.SG.PRES  put  to  cry-INF
  'She started to cry'

We may conclude, then, that from the earliest records, Acadian French has exhibited *avoir* selection with pronominal verbs.

Auxiliary selection has been the object of a number of full-scale quantitative studies in the North American context, for both Laurentian and Acadian varieties. Table 5.1 gives an overview of findings for Laurentian varieties spoken in Quebec City (Beniak and Mougeon 1989), Montreal (Sankoff and Thibault 1977), Ottawa-Hull (Willis 2000), Vermont (Russo and Roberts 1999), along with Acadian varieties spoken in Nova Scotia (Gesner 1979b), New Brunswick (Péronnet 1991), and Prince Eward Island (King

TABLE 5.1

Proportion of avoir Use with Verbs Which Select être in Standard French

| Verbs | Ottawa-Hull | Quebec City | Hawkes-bury | Vermont | Communities Montreal | N.S. | N.B. | P.E.I. |
|---|---|---|---|---|---|---|---|---|
| aller[a] | | | 22% | 30% 29/97 | 0.7% 3/404 | * | * | * |
| arriver | 43% 125/294 | 10% | 60% | 31% 11/36 | 11% 45/426 | 100% 5/5 | 100% 42/42 | 100% 112/112 |
| déménager | 84% 105/125 | | | 73% 16/22 | 69% 70/102 | | | 100% 9/9 |
| demeurer | 89% 16/18 | | | 85% 17/20 | 90% 69/77 | *** | *** | *** |
| descendre | 59% 13/22 | 67% | 91% | | 50% 8/16 | | 100% 3/3 | 100% 10/10 |
| devenir | 12% 2/17 | | | | | | | 100% 5/5 |
| entrer | 50% 3/6 | | | | 6% 1/16 | | | 100% 9/9 |
| monter | 92% 36/39 | 33% | 100% | 78% 25/32 | 68% 19/28 | 100% 1/1 | | 100% 12/12 |
| partir | 66% 84/128 | 9% | 41% | 54% 25/46 | 36% 54/148 | 100% 1/1 | 100% 12/12 | 94% 34/36 |
| passer | 91% 90/99 | 100% | 100% | 50% 5/10 | 90% 92/102 | 100% 1/1 | 100% 8/8 | 100% 43/43 |
| rentrer | 84% 79/94 | 50% | 83% | 55% 6/11 | 74% 68/92 | 100% 2/2 | 100% 8/8 | 100% 26/26 |
| rester | 93% 56/60 | 33% | 82% | 71% 24/34 | 70% 238/338 | 100% 6/6 | | 100% 97/97 |
| retourner | 60% 24/40 | 33% | 75% | 90% 9/10 | 46% 17/37 | | | 100% 6/6 |
| revenir | 24% 18/74 | 7% | | | 5% 4/76 | 100% 2/2 | | 100% 13/13 |
| sortir | 81% 80/99 | 29% | 74% | 75% 18/24 | 69% 70/102 | 100% ? | 100% 12/12 | 100% 35/35 |
| tomber | 88% 50/57 | 62% | 92% | 85% 17/20 | 72% 48/67 | 100% 1/1 | | 100% 7/7 |
| venir | 20% 62/309 | 24% | 63% | 24% 19/78 | 7% 24/341 | 100% 19/19 | 100% 39/39 | 99% 204/207 |
| pron. v's | | 6% | 31% | | | 100% 27/27 | 100% 103/103 | 100% 175/175 |

SOURCE: Ottawa-Hull (Willis 2000); Quebec City (Beniak and Mougeon (1989); Ontario (Beniak and Mougeon 1989); Vermont (Russo and Roberts 1999); Montreal (Sankoff and Thibault 1977); Nova Scotia (Gesner 1979b); Nouveau-Brunswick (Péronnet 1991), and Prince Edward Island (King and Nadasdi 2005).

a. The absence of data for *aller* for the Acadian studies is due to the fact that in these varieties, *été*, not *allé*, is the past participle of *aller*. *J'ai été* 'lit. I have been', along with all other person/number conjugations, only allow auxiliary *avoir*.

and Nadasdi 2005). It is likewise the only auxiliary verb used with unaccusatives and pronominal verbs in the entire L'Anse-à-Canards corpus. All of the corpora represented in table 5.1 show substantial usage of the *avoir* auxiliary where Standard French would have *être*. It is in the Acadian context—in Péronnet's (1991) and Gesner's (1979b) studies of older speakers and in King and Nadasdi's (2005) study involving a wide age range—that *avoir* approaches categoriality. Further, use of *avoir* extends categorically to pronominal verbs in the corpora consulted, the very context which either goes unremarked on in other studies of North American French (Sankoff and Thibault 1977; Russo and Roberts 1999; Willis 2000) or shows a proportion of *avoir* use that is small (Beniak and Mougeon 1989).[6] Examples (2)–(4) illustrate auxiliary selection found in the Prince Edward Island corpus, with intransitive verbs in (2), *tomber* 'to fall', and (3), *partir* 'to leave', and with a pronominal verb in (4), *se dégreyér* 'to get undressed'.

2. *Ils      aviont         tombé dans l'  eau.*
   they   have-3PL.IMP fell     in    the  water
   'They had fallen into the water'

3. *J'   ai              parti en 1960 puis l'   électricité  a*
   1PERS have.1SG.PRES left  in  1960 and  the  electricity  have.3SG.PRES
   *venu   après.*
   came   after
   'I left in 1960 and the electricity came after'

4. *Je    m'   ai              toute dégreyé.[7]*
   1PERS REFL have.1SG.PRES all    undressed
   'I got all undressed'

Further, Giancarli's (2011) reports that in Péronnet's 1985 75,000 word corpus for seven rural southeastern New Brunswick speakers, only 3 of 176 tokens (1.7%) of auxiliary usage with pronominal verbs involve *être*. Péronnet (1991) herself cites examples such as (5) and (6):

5. *I'   s'    avont         préparé.*
   they REFL have-3PL.PRES prepared
   'They got themselves ready'

6. *Quand que la  vieille     s'    a              levé, le  gars*
   when  that the old.woman REFL have.SG.PRES risen the guy
   *était        parti*
   be-SG.IMP left
   'When the old woman got up, the guy had left'

However, as was noted above, two of the largest extant compora for contemporary French—the Sankoff/Cedergren Montreal 1971 corpus and the Poplack 1982 Ottawa-Hull corpus—contain no attestations of such usage. Likewise, Seutin's (1975, 286–89) study of the variety spoken on Îles-aux-Coudres, in the St. Lawrence River, found variable auxiliary selection with unaccusatives but not with pronominal verbs, where only *être* was found. This is an important result because this island community existed in relative isolation over the course of the centuries. On the basis of the Laurentian documentation and the Acadian-Laurentian contrasts in table 5.1, one might hypothesize that use of *avoir* had actually spread to pronominal verbs in the New World. However, this hypothesis would be contradicted by Frei's (1929) early-twentieth-century observations, along with Grevisse's (1969) commentary on early use of *avoir* in this context and the relevant twentieth-century European French dialectal data.

The question now becomes one of why pronominal verb use of *avoir* has only rarely been attested in Laurentian varieties. Rideout (2011) has argued that such use of *avoir* was singled out for stigmatization in the sixteenth century, at a time when the French norm became centered on the speech of the Paris higher classes. Rideout contrasts the commentary of two sixteenth-century grammarians, John Palsgrave (1530) and Gilles du Wes (1532). Although published just two years apart, they differ dramatically in their treatment of auxiliaries. Palsgrave, strongly influenced by the emerging Parisian norm and by the written language, presents auxiliary alternation, while du Wes, a native speaker from the Picardy region who based his grammar on actual spoken usage, presents only *avoir*, including with pronominal verbs.

Palgrave's style of grammar would win out, and, not surprisingly, use of *avoir* with pronominal verbs disappears from most grammatical commentary.[8] When we return to the *Atlas linguistique de la France* (Gilliéron and Édmont 1902–10) and look at the actual source areas for Laurentian settlement—Normandy, the center-west, and Île-de-France (which includes Paris)—we find attestations of *être* with pronominal verbs between the Loire and the Seine Rivers, an area that includes Île-de-France. Du Wes's Picardy and Palsgrave's Île-de-France thus look rather different in the dialect literature of almost three centuries later with regard to this particular verb type.

The settlers of New France were socially diverse as well as geographically diverse. They came from a range of social classes (Charbonneau and Guillemette 1994), while most Acadian settlers were members of the lower class, originating in the center-west (Massignon 1962). As discussed in chapter 2, the New France (later Quebec) settlers generally had greater access to education across the centuries than did the Acadians. We may thus appeal to the same line of reasoning invoked by King, Martineau, and Mougeon (2011) to explain the rarity of first-person plural *je… ons* in these same Laurentian varieties. That is, we may hypothesize that just as a highly salient pronominal variant (i.e., first-person plural *je* accompanied by the *-ons* ending on the verb, e.g., *je parlons* 'I speak') may have been lost, so, too, would *avoir* auxiliary usage marked (or triggered) by pronominal verbs (e.g., *se lever* 'to get (oneself) up'), present in some but not all of the source varieties. In contrast, both vernacular variants have thrived in Acadian communities where contact with speakers of other varieties of French has historically been quite limited.

In Canale et al.'s (1977) study of adolescent language use in the Ontario towns of Welland, Sudbury, and Rayside, *avoir* was found to be the majority variant with intransitives such as *tomber* 'to fall', *rentrer* 'to come hone', *rester* 'to stay', *sortir* 'to leave', and *venir* 'to come'.[9] These researchers also uncovered 27% *avoir* use (*n* = 37) with pronominal verbs. As the total number of occurrences for this variable is low, the authors do not break the data down by community. All are, and were, minority francophone communities. What we cannot tell is whether use of *avoir* with pronominal verbs is in this case a recent regularization or one also (strongly) present in the speech of older generations of Franco-Ontarians. However, it is clear that the social situation of French in these communities is more similar to the Acadian context than that of the Quebec communities studied in that normative pressure is lower.

The story does not end there, however. In the case of auxiliary selection, we are able to examine variation (and perhaps change) introduced by the educational system, specifically efforts at the Université de Moncton, where since 1999 all undergraduate students have had to take a minimum of six credits in French (the equivalent of one academic year) to improve their skills in normative French. Balcom's (2008) study compares usage on experimental tasks of first-year students who had not yet completed such a course and fourth-year students who had. The dependent variable was auxiliary selection: in both a controlled-production (fill in the blanks) task and an acceptability judgment task, the fourth-year students did exhibit some variation between vernacular and normative usage but significantly less than did first-year students. Their usage of *être* with pronominal verbs was, however, categorical in this formal context. Such a course involves the introduction of an auxiliary contrast with unaccusatives not present in earlier stages of the variety and its antecedents: it brings supralocal variants of the variable into prominence, much as in the Esch (2002) study of change across the lifespan, cited above.[10] In a similar vein, Sankoff, Thibault, and Wagner's (2004) found that individuals who participated in the Montreal 1971 corpus who had achieved high levels of education and professional status used *être* at much higher rates when they were reinterviewed some 25 years later.

Patterns of auxiliary selection, then, involve the interplay of many factors: regional variation in France, degree of isolation, degree of normative pressure in the New World, and degree of saliency of the verb type. There is some evidence that Laurentian varieties spoken in minority settings are moving in the Acadian direction. On the other hand, we also see newly emergent variation emerging as a result of another type of dialect contact, in the broad sense of the term, in the Moncton setting. Finally, on both sides of the Atlantic, there is evidence of change across the lifespan.

## ORPHAN PREPOSITIONS AND THE EMERGENCE OF PREPOSITION STRANDING

In the remainder of this chapter, I consider a phenomenon not typically associated with the French language: preposition stranding, that is, the movement of a *wh*-phrase object of a preposition to the specifier of CP, leaving behind a "stranded" preposition (and, within the Minimalist tradition, an unpronounced copy of the *wh*-phrase). In an article with Yves Roberge published more than 20 years ago (King and Roberge 1990), we documented stranding in canonical "movement" constructions: in *wh*-questions (7), relatives (8), and pseudo-passives (9):

7. *Quoi  ce-que  tu     travailles        dessus?* [11]
   what  that   you   work.SG.PRES  on
   'What are you working on?'

8. *Lui,  c'   est           le    gars  que   je       travaille        pour.*
   him  he  be.3SG.PRES  the  guy  that  1PERS  work.SG.PRES  for
   'Him, he's the guy I work for'

9. *Le   ciment   a             été    marché  dedans  avant   d'  être    sec.*
   the  concrete  have.3SG.PRES  been  walked  in          before  of  be-INF  dry
   'The concrete was walked on before being dry'

For the francophone, and indeed for speakers of any number of languages, these data are striking, given that very few of the world's languages (only English and the mainland Scandinavian languages, along with members of the Kru family) have this option. Since preposition stranding is not documented for European French nor is it documented for many Laurentian varieties, this is clearly a New World innovation.

Now, in some discourse contexts, the presposition may occur without an overt complement in French; the missing object has been variously analyzed as occurring when the preposition is used as an adverb (Grevisse 1986), as recoverable through discourse linking (Martinet 1979), as resulting from deletion (Arrivé, Gadet, and Galmiche 1986) or as pro (Tuller 1986; Zribi-Hertz 1984). The examples in (10)–(12) are from Grevisse (1986, 1509; cited by Roberge and Rosen 1999):

10. *et    vous   coulez          avec*
    and   you    sink-2PL.PRES   with
    'and you sink with (it)'

11. *Tu    n'    es              pas    fait    pour.*
    you   NEG   be.2SG.PRES    NEG    made   for
    'You are not made for (it)'

12. *Il    a              écrit     des    poèmes   avec   rimes   et    des*
    he    have.3SG.PRES   written   some   poems    with   rhymes  and   some
    *poèmes   sans.*
    poems    without
    'He has written poems with rhymes and poems without (them)'

Working within the generative framework of the period, King and Roberge (1990) perform a number of diagnostic tests to show that data like (6)–(9) do actually involve *wh*-movement; that is, they are different in kind from the data in (10)–(12). We go on to consider why *wh*-movement has actually developed in Prince Edward Island French, at that time not known to exist in any Romance language. We linked the emergence of the movement option to the borrowing of English prepositions in Prince Edward Island French: it turned out that the Prince Edward Island corpus contains numerous combinations of French verb + English-origin presposition (e.g., *parler about* 'to talk about'), English-origin verb + English preposition (e.g., *layer off* 'to lay off (from work)'), and English-origin verb + French preposition (*crasher dedans* 'to crash into'). Native-speaker intuitions judged all of the constructed data found in (13)–(15) to be grammatical.

13. *Quoi   ce-qu'   ils    parlont        about?*
    what   that     they   talk-3PL.PRES   about
    'What are they talking about?'

14. *Qui    ce-qu'   a               été    layé    off?*
    who    that     have.3SG.PRES   been   laid    off
    'Who were laid off?'

15. *Quoi-   ce que   l'    avion      a               crashé    dedans?*
    what    that    the   airplane   have.3SG.PRES   crashed   into
    'What did the airplane crash into?'

In subsequent work (King 2000), I determined that the Prince Edward Island corpora, for Abram-Village and Saint-Louis, show 67 different verb + preposition combinations, comprising 17% of the English-origin verbs ($n = 2,349$). Note as well that English-origin verbs, as is usually the case in French, are morphologically integrated into the host language, as shown in (14) and (15). These data all show what is typically referred to as verb + particle constructions in traditional grammars; following on work by Emonds (1976), I categorize these structures as involving intransitive prepositions.

Stowell (1981, 1982) makes the interesting observation that languages which allow preposition stranding also allow this construction (though the reverse is not necessarily true), and the PEI facts are certainly in keeping with this generalization. Following on Longobardi's (2001; see also Keenan 2002) call for a focus on determining causation in cases of syntactic change (rather than simply documenting such change and/or appealing to traditional notions like drift), I then investigated the behavior of prepositions in all of the Acadian varieties, as well as the Laurentian varieties for which I could access data.

Before we embark on cross-varietal comparisons, Rowlett's (2007, 60, n. 60) observation that "[i]n Contemporary French preposition stranding is found, at least in relative clauses, e.g., *le mec que je t'ai vu avec*" needs qualifying. This relative clause structure (the example here would be translated into English as "the guy that I saw you with") has been categorized as a case of stranding by a number of earlier researchers. However, Bouchard (1982), Vinet (1984), and Zribi-Hertz (1984) all present convincing evidence that this is, in fact, a relative clause of the resumptive pronoun type (they argue that the empty complement position is occupied by pro). In fact, Bouchard suggests that such structures are not innovations in contemporary French, but rather may be found in the language as early as the fourteenth century. Thus, the structure Rowlett (and others) identify as preposition stranding would be more properly categorized as involving an orphan preposition (without movement of an operator). The French facts we will consider below are also relevant to recent theorizing on preposition stranding: for instance, Law (1998, 2006) hypothesizes that the existence of suppletive forms of P + D, like French *de + le > du*, prevents preposition stranding in a language (i.e., pied-piping of the complement of the preposition would be obligatory). However, just such suppletive forms exist in Prince Edward Island French, and indeed in all of the varieties of French to be discussed below, casting doubt on Law's hypothesis.

The data considered so far involve prepositions with lexical content involving spatial or directional relations (e.g., *dans ~ dedans* 'in', *su ~ dessus* 'on', etc.), as do the prepositions of English origin found in the corpus (*about, along, around, back, down, off, on, out, over, through,* and *up*). Stranding is also seen with *pour* 'for' and *avec* 'with', both French-origin prepositions with lexical content. We may consider data like *Qui as-tu voté pour?* 'Who did you vote for?' as an instance of calquing, which, like lexical borrowing, involves the featural properties of lexical items, in this case French *pour* 'for'. In addition, more purely grammatical prepositions may also be stranded in Prince Edward Island French, including *à* and *de*, illustrated in (16) and (17):

16. *Où ce-qu' elle vient de?*
    where that she come.SG.PRES from
    'Where is she from?'

17. *Quelle heure qu' il a arrivé à?*
    what time that he have.SG.PRES arrived at
    'What time did he arrive?'

The English equivalents of *à* 'to' and *de* 'of' (or in some cases 'from', as above) do not occur in verb + preposition constructions, although *parler about* (in 13 above) could in fact be rendered as *parler de*. Thus, the Prince Edward Island varieties show that a preposition's ability to be stranded has arguably been extended from borrowed English-origin prepositions to French prepositions in general.

Roberge and Rosen's (1999) follow-up to the original Acadian French article observed that in Sainte-Lina, Alberta (Laurentian), French (pers. comm. to the authors by Rose-Marie Déchaine), along with Louisiana French (based on Stäbler 1995), allowed preposition stranding similar to Prince Edward Island French, but not with complements of *à* and *de*. As Roberge and Rosen point out, *à* and *de* assign Case to their complements, but no thematic role. Further, prepositions that appear without a phonologically realized complement likewise do not assign Case (i.e., *dessus, dedans*, along with *avec* used in a detransitived position in a context such as *le gars que je sors avec* 'the guy I go out with'; see Rowlett 2007, and above). On the basis of these dialectal distinctions and the technical apparatus made available within the Principles and Parameters framework, Roberge and Rosen (1999, 159) argue that what is at issue for varieties allowing stranding is "a shift in the prepositional system such that the [−Case] paradigm has become part of the [+Case] one." This would account for their Alberta French and Louisiana French data. As for the Prince Edward Island French facts, the grammar underlying them would have stranding extended to the [−θ, +Case] prepositions *à* and *de*. Roberge and Rosen thus provide a feature-driven account of dialectal variation in the spirit of much recent work in generative grammar.

Let's now consider other varieties of North American French spoken in contact with English, beginning with the other Acadian varieties for which we have data. Roy (1979) found a number of other prepositions of English origin in the Moncton, New Brunswick, corpus (she cites *about, on*, and *off* [68]), and also gives the following examples of orphan French prepositions that arguably involve stranding (60):

18. *C' est la chose que je veux vous parler de.*
    it be.3SG.PRES the thing that 1PERS want.SG.PRES you speak-INF of
    'It's the thing I want to talk to you about'

19. *Si  que  la  personne  j'  ai  adressée...  je  m'*
    if  that  the  person  1PERS  have.1SG.PRES  addressed  1PERS  REFL
    *ai  adressé  à  peut  pas  me  comprendre...*
    have.SG.PRES  addressed  to  can.3SG.PRES  NEG  me  understand-INF
    'If the person I speak to ... I speak to cannot understand me...'

A number of more recent studies have provided southeastern New Brunswick data that look like those for Prince Edward Island, including Perrot
(1995) and Young (2002), both doctoral dissertations. One of Young's adolescent consultants provides us with a striking example of an English origin
verb + preposition construction in (20):

20. *Ça  m'  a  totally  turné  off  la  dope.*
    it  me  have.SG.PRES  totally  turned  off  the  dope
    'It totally turned me off dope'

Chevalier and Long's (2005) study is based on data from three small corpora for the southeast (Anna-Malenfant 1994; Parkton 1994; *chiac*-Kaspar-
ian 1999), all involving adolescent speakers. Chevalier and Long found
seven English-origin prepositions in these corpora: *back, out, up, off, on, in,*
and *around*, overlapping with the Prince Edward Island set given above.
Putting these materials together, we may assume that the southeastern New
Brunswick variety behaves like the Prince Edward Island ones, and, given
the mid-1970s date of Roy's data collection (and the fairly wide age range
of her sample), that the phenomenon is not limited to adolescent speech.

    As for the Nova Scotia varieties, Flikeid (1989a) provides several exam-
ples showing stranding, including the example in (21):

21. Ils allont out, zeux chuckont leurs...leurs scallops out.
    they go-3PL.PRES out them shuck-3PL.PRES their their scallops out
    'They go out, they chuck their, their scallops out'

So, too, does the Butler Sociolinguistic Corpus for Grosses Coques, which
shows that stranding extends to *à* and *de* in this variety.

22. *...asteure  que  je  sons  movés  out  du  logis.*
    now  that  1PERS  be.1PL.PRES  moved  out  of.the  house
    '...now that they are moved out of the house'

23. SPEAKER A: *Je  ferai  jamais  ça.*
    1PERS  do.1SG.FUT  never  that
    'I'll never do that'[12]

    SPEAKER B: *Oh, tu,  tu  es  point  allowée  de.*
    oh  you  you  be.2SG.PRES  NEG  allowed  of
    'Oh, you, you are not allowed to'

However, in the Newfoundland varieties we see little evidence of either prepositions of English origin or stranding. For instance, Prince Edward Island French *Où ce-qu'elle vient de?* would be rendered *D'où ce-qu'elle vient?* with pied-piping or *Elle vient d'où?* with *wh*-in-situ. Preposition stranding involving *wh*-interrogatives is limited to particular calqued verb + preposition combinations (e.g., *voter pour* 'to vote for'). In fact, the L'Anse-à-Canards corpora includes telling examples like (24):

24. *Il    a              fait    give   up.*
    he   have.SG.PRES   made   give   up
    'He gave up'

Here a *faire* + infinitive construction "eases" English *give up* (arguably a code-switch) into the discourse; in other Acadian varieties, morphologically incorporated *giver up* would be the norm, particularly for in-group usage such as is the case here.

As for northeastern New Brunswick, recall from chapter 2 that there is a very high level of francophone presence, indeed monolingual francophone presence, in this area of the province. It does not present the right conditions for borrowing prepositions of English origin, then, any more than does the neighboring area of Quebec. In fact, Beaulieu (pers. comm., Apr. 2, 2007) reports only 4 instances of (locative) *back* in 100 hours of recording for 16 speakers in the Français acadien du nord-est du Nouveau Brunswick (FANENB) corpus, recorded in the early 1990s. Occurrence of *back* turns out to be a good diagnostic for degree of English influence: *back* is a very old, well-established borrowing of North American French, and if it is not present, or barely present, we would not expect to find other prepositions of English origin.

What of the Louisiana varieties? First, recall from chapter 3 that verbs of English origin are not morphologically incorporated in this variety but occur in their bare forms. The one preposition of English origin that I know to occur relatively frequently in Louisiana French is *back* (example taken from Rottet 2000, 120; cited by King 2011).[13]

25. *Après   mon   pape   s'      a                        mouri   dans   '84,   on*
    after   my    father   REFL   have.3SG.PRES   died   in      '84    one
    *a                        pris    back   la      maison.*
    have.3SG.PRES   taken   back   the   house
    'After my father died in '84, we took back the house'

Rottet (2001, 232–33) does note, however, that younger speakers have begun to use more strong pronoun forms, as in (26) and (27), as well as to exhibit increased frequency of preposition omission, as in (28) and (29) (Rottet's examples 14, 15, 17, and 18, respectively, presented in the original orthography).[14]

26. *Que ça c' est         le   tiroir   que  vous gardez         votres*
    that this it be.3SG.PRES the  drawer  that you  keep-2PL.PRES your
    *cuillières dedans?*[15]
    spoons     in
    'Is this the drawer you keep your spoons in?'

27. *Il     ont            besoin d' un  bol   pour       mettre   du*
    they   have.3PL.PRES  need   of a   bowl  in.order.to put-INF some
    *ponche dedans.*[16]
    punch  in
    'They need a bowl to put punch in'

28. *Ça, c' est le  tiroir   que  vous gardez         votres   cuillières Ø?*
    that it is  the drawer   that you  keep-2PL.PRES  your.PL  spoons
    'Is this the drawer that you keep your spoons?'

29. *Il     ont            besoin d' un  bol   pour       mettre   le*
    they   have.3PL.PRES  need   of a   bowl  in.order.to put-INF some
    *ponche Ø.*
    punch
    'They need a bowl to put punch (in)'

Somewhat surprisingly, Rottet (2001, 233) cites preposition stranding with *à* as a feature avoided by younger speakers of this Louisiana variety. He gives the example in (30) (his 20), noting that the structure was used once by one speaker of the oldest age group (55+ in 1993) in his study: his other speakers used preposition omission for such cases, as in (27) and (28), or substituted a strong pronoun. For instance, in a case where the target utterance is *être content de* 'to be proud of', several speakers used *être content après* or *être content pour* (the latter would normally involve being proud 'for someone'). Rottet also gives one example of stranded *de*, reproduced as (31) (2001, 168, ex. 93), as well as stranded *à*, shown in (30):

30. *Jha c' est         le   magasin que  je vas           tout le  temps*
    that it be.3SG.PRES the  store   that I  go.SG.PRES    all  the time
    *à.*
    to
    'That, that's the store that I always go to'

31. ... *une    bête    Cadien    qu'    a                été    électé    en place*
    a      stupid  Cajun    who    have.SG.PRES    been   elected   in place
    *est            après    changer        tout  la    mode qu'    eusses  avait*
    be.3SG.PRES   after    change-INF    all   the   way   that   them   have.SG.IMP
    *l'    habitude  de.*
    the   habit     of
    '...a dumb Cajun who was elected to office is changing the way that they
    are used to'

Rottet (2001, 233) interprets his consultants' generational increase in the
use of strong pronouns and other strategies of avoiding weak pronouns as in
accordance with "the well-known tendency that speakers with restricted language input, like terminal speakers of a dying language, have [for] salient,
marked forms and analytic syntax [...] English influence [...] serves to
reinforce the preference for stranding." We see, then, that the interpretation of a particular example (like 30 or 31) differs markedly depending on
the characteristics of the speech community: the Acadians whose speech
has been described up to this point are all fluent, albeit bilingual, speakers
of French.

We are still left with an important question. In a situation of intense
language contact and low normative pressure, why do we not see integration of prepositions of English origin into the Louisiana variety described
by Rottet? I believe the answer goes back once again to the breakdown of
verbal morphology: if English prepositions typically enter French in combination with verbs of English origin, in collocations such as *giver up*, *shutter
down*, and *turner out*, a grammar must be available to support their integration. In other words, if verbs of English origin are not integrated into the
grammar (and their lack of French verbal morphology is clear evidence of
this), how could their accompanying prepositions be?

We turn finally to variation in Laurentian French. Roberge and Rosen
(1999) assert that the only pattern it shares with Acadian French is the use
of strong pronouns with relative clauses, as in (8) above. The structure of
data like these would differ from one variety to the other, though: Bouchard
(1982) and Vinet (1984) show that subjacency requirements do not apply
to Quebec French relative clauses, whereas King and Roberge (1990) show
that they actually do in Prince Edward Island French.[17] So Quebec French
arguably does not have *wh*-movement in any of the key environments tested
above. I note as well that while Quebec French, like Newfoundland French,
borrows verbs from English, they do not borrow prepositions: verb + preposition structures like those illustrated above are not found, and neither is
preposition stranding.

When we turn to Laurentian varieties spoken in western Canada, we find intercommunity variation. While Roberge and Rosen (1999) suggest that the Sainte-Lina, Alberta, variety does not exhibit stranding of *à* and *de*, Walker's (2004, 56) description of the Rivière-la-Paix, Alberta, variety suggests that this one does:

32.  *C' était     quoi...,  comme  que   tu    veux        jamais  t'en*
     it be.SG.IMP  what      like   that  you   want.SG.PRES ever    REFL
     *souvenir      de?*
     remember-INF  of
     'It was what ... like you never want to remember?'

French is in a minority position in western Canada, as it is all provinces west of Quebec, and normative French would have little impact in these small Alberta communities. It is most likely that, while grammatical judgments alone (for Sainte-Lina) or a small descriptive study (for Rivière-la-Paix) may tell us what sorts of structures are available to speakers, they do not tell us their distribution in the community.

Recent developments in the Welsh language provide some support for the analysis of Acadian French outlined here. It turns out that late-twentieth-century Welsh developed verb + particle constructions (calqued on English, see Rottet 2000, 2005). Recent work on Welsh syntax shows that the language has acquired preposition stranding (Willis 2000, 557; Borsley, Tallerman, and Willis 2007, 116). Thus, we find evidence in favor of another contact-based account of the emergence of preposition stranding, one that turns on acquiring verb + particle (i.e., intransitive preposition) combinations. The borrowing of such collocations thus appears to be a necessary (but necessarily a sufficient) condition for acquiring preposition stranding.

## CONCLUSION

In this chapter, we have examined in some detail two changes involving small sets of lexical items. With regard to auxiliary selection, quantitative analyses have been particularly useful in teasing apart differences among varieties, while the traditional dialect literature has helped provide explanations for these differences. With regard to the structural properties of prepositions, quantitative analysis for the Prince Edward Island varieties laid the basis for cross-varietal comparisons. In both cases, the Acadian facts have allowed us to understand grammatical developments on a larger scale, from both synchronic and diachronic perspectives.

# 6. EXPRESSIVITY AND INNOVATION

IN THE PRECEDING CHAPTERS, we have encountered a number of changes involving simplification of the grammar, such as the emergence and spread of yes/no questions with the question marker *ti/tu* (chapter 4), a less "costly" operation than pronominal inversion in terms of principle of economy. In the present chapter, I consider the role of discourse in linguistic innovation, specifically due to the drive for expressivity, a tendency that competes with simplification in linguistic change (see Martinet 1955, among others). To consider examples of expressivity and innovation, we need look no further than the use of intensifiers in a language. For instance, Denison and Hogg (2006) have noted for the history of English that the drive for expressivity explains the fairly rapid turnover of intensifiers: by way of example, they discuss *terribly, real, dead, way, well,* and the like in British English.[1] They make the point that once the originally hyperbolic nature of a particular intensifier begins to wane, the process begins again, with the introduction of new intensifiers. In this chapter, we will first consider turnover of intensifiers in the Acadian context, which will lead to a discussion of borrowings from English. Next, we turn to two cases of innovation involving another type of bilingual discourse phenomena—the use of English-origin discourse markers and evidential expressions—considering both social and linguistic mechanisms of integration and reanalysis. I argue that all these cases of innovation can be viewed as motivated by expressivity, which may go on to affect the host grammar.

## INTENSIFIERS IN ACADIAN FRENCH

The Acadian French corpora considerd here contain a variety of intensifiers, including some found in many other varieties of French, such as *mortellement* 'deadly'. *Le Grand Robert* etymological dictionary of the French language (2nd ed., 1985) gives attestations from the fourteenth century in which *mortellement* is used with its original, literal meaning, along with non-literal attestations such as *mortellement ennuyeux* 'deadly boring', dating from the nineteenth century. Since usage of *mortellement* as an intensifier is attested in both Acadian and Laurentian varieties, we may assume that figurative usage likely developed much earlier in the language than is found in the citations in *Le Grand Robert*. The example in (1) is taken from the Prince Edward Island corpus.

1. *L'   église   est              mortellement belle.*
  the   church   be.3SG.PRES deadly          beautiful
  'The church is really beautiful'

Another French adverb which taks the *-ment* derivational suffix, *moyen-nement* 'fairly' (e.g., *moyennement beau* 'fairly handsome'), is also attested in *Le Grand Robert* and other European documentation and in Laurentian sources such as the *Trésor de la langue française au Québec*.[2] However, in Baie Sainte-Marie Acadian French, *moyennement*, pronounced [mwenmã] or [mwemã] by elderly mid-twentieth-century speakers (Philip Comeau, pers. comm., Apr. 20, 2012), is now pronounced [wɛlmã]. Dissimilation (m→l/_n) is a natural phonological process, as is the loss of initial /m/ before the glide. Most interesting is the adverb's semantic reanalysis in this particular variety: today native speakers write the adverb as *wellment* and assign it much more force than *moyennement*. For current Baie Sainte-Marie Acadian French, *wellment* should be glossed as 'really', as in the example below from the Grosses Coques corpus.

2. *Ça,   c' est              wellment beau.*
  that it be.3SG.PRES really    beautiful
  'That, that's really beautiful'

The choice of orthography here is in line with native speaker interpretation of *moyennement* [wɛlmã] as a borrowing from English, noted above. Although the historical record does not show a stage where the phonological changes appear with the original meaning ('fairly') intact, the phonological realignment of *moyennement* with English *well* + *-ment* arguably led to its semantic reanalysis. Interestingly, *mortellement* is not found in the Grosses Coques corpus nor is it recognized as traditional to the Baie Sainte-Marie variety by native speakers. This does not mean that the variety rejects synonymy, since there is another variation on *moyennement*, *wayment*, morphologically integrated into French and used with exactly the same meaning as *wellment*:[3]

3. *Hier,   il   a              wayment venté.*
  yesterday it have.3SG.PRES really    blown
  'Yesterday, it was really windy'

Such data exploit the morphology of French adverb formation with *-ment*, which we normally associate with turning adjectives into adverbs (e.g., *douce-ment* 'softly', *certainement* 'certainly', *heureusement* 'happily') or with creating new adverbs from existing ones (e.g., *quasi* 'almost' > *quasiment* 'almost, practically').

4. *C' était        quasiment toute des      prêtres de      France.*
   it be.3SG.IMP almost     all   some priests from France
   'It was almost all priests from France'

I find no mention of *wellment* or *wayment* in the extant literature on Acadian French. However, a number of researchers (Perrot 1995; Young 2002; Chevalier and Hudson 2005) discuss use of English *right* in sociolinguistic interviews with Moncton, New Brunswick, adolescents. The example in (5) is taken from Perrot, while (6) is from Young.

5. *J'        ai            right aimé ça.*
   1PERS have.1SG.PRES right liked that
   'I really liked that'
6. *Moi, je      demande    comme des    fois    là    comme pas   right*
   me   1PERS ask-SG.PRES like    some times there like    NEG right
   *souvent.*
   often
   'I ask, like, sometimes, like, not very often'

Since I do not have access to the corpora on which these studies are based, I cannot state positively that these lexical items are borrowings rather than single-word code-switches.[4]

However, Chevalier and Hudson (2005, 292) do discuss *right*'s syntactic integration into the host language, one diagnostic for borrowing status. For instance, they cite parallel French structures to (7)'s use of *right*, given in (8).

7. *A   i       donne      right beaucoup de      cadeaux.*[5]
   she her.DAT give.SG.PRES right a.lot    of    gifts
   'She gave her quite a lot of gifts'
8. *Elle lui      donne         vraiment/énormément de      cadeaux.*
   she her.DAT give.SG.PRES many/a.lot           PART gifts
   'She gave her a lot of gifts'

Intensifier *right* is also attested in the Grosses Coques corpus, shown in (9).[6]

9. *Ils   restiont      right proche à   York University.*
   they stay-3PL.IMP right close to York University
   'They were living really close to York University'

Both Chevalier and Hudson (2005) and Burnett (2008) draw our attention to the fact that not only Acadian varieties borrow intensifiers from English. They point to use of *full* by young Quebec adolescents, as in (10) and (11) (from Chevalier and Hudson 2005, 295):

10. *J'      aime        full   ça.*
    1PERS  like.SG.PRES  full   that
    'I really like that'

11. *J'      ai          full   mangé.*
    1PERS  have.SG.PRES  full   eaten
    'I ate a lot'

Finally, there is a related usage to what we have seen in the above discussion in the Baie Sainte-Marie variety: this concerns *quite*, used as a degree word in English (e.g., *quite expensive*) and also as a peripheral modifier (*quite a bad grade*). Huddleston and Pullum (2002, 721) argue that the first use of *quite* is at the top of any degree scale; indeed, it is probably equivalent to French *extrêmement* 'extremely'. As a degree word, *quite* would uncontroversially occupy the specifier position ('sister of X') of the category it modifies (e.g., AP, in the example cited above, or an AdvP, as in *quite slowly*). As a peripheral modifier, however, it must occur before the article in a noun phrase (e.g., *quite a show*, *\*a quite show*); its semantics involves reinforcement. This latter usage thus differs from APs that contain degree adverbs, which may both precede and follow the determiner (e.g., *more serious a problem* or, in canonical AP position, a *more serious problem*).[7]

Consider English *quite* in comparison with the usage illustrated in the data in (12)–(14), from the Grosses Coques corpus. Here *quite* resembles the English peripheral modifier more so than the specifier, in that while it involves reinforcement it does not modify an adverb or adjective. However, note that in this Acadian French variety the syntax of *quite* differs markedly from English. *Une quite de visite* (12) can only be rendered 'quite a visit' in English, whereas a close reading of the surrounding text in (13) leads me to translate *C'était une quite de Joanne* as 'Joan was quite something'.

12. *Vous aviez           fait   une  quite  de  visite.*
    you    have-2PL.IMP   made   a    quite  of  visit
    'You had had quite a visit'

13. *J'      avons        eu   un  quite  de  souper  hier       à     soir,*
    1PERS  have-1PL.PRES  had  a   quite  of  supper  yesterday  at    night
    *nous-  autres.*
    us     others
    'We had quite a supper last night, us'

14. SPEAKER A: *Elle a                 eu   une  vingtaine               d'*
                she  have.3SG.PRES     had  a    twenty.approximate      PART
                *opérations. Elle a              été    hachouillé  all   over.*
                operations  she  have.3SG.PRES  been   lacerated   all   over
                'She had about twenty operations. She was lacerated all over.'

SPEAKER B: *Oui. C' était      une quite  de  Joanne.   God damn...*
           yes  it  be.SG.IMP  a    quite of  Joanne   God damn
           'Yes. Joanne is quite something. God damn...'

While it is impossible to insert an adjectival modifier before Baie Sainte-
Marie Acadian *quite*, as illustrated in (15), it is possible to insert one before
the noun at the right edge of the phrase, as in (16) (Philip Comeau, pers.
comm., Apr. 20, 2012):

15. *\*J'      avons             eu   un  bon   quite  de  souper.*
     1PERS have-1PL.PRES  had  a   good  quite of  supper
     'We had quite a good supper'

16. *J'      avons                  eu   un  quite  de  bon      souper.*
     1PERS have-1PL.PRES  NEG  had  a   quite of  good   supper
     *'We had quite a good supper'

These data look very much like the construction exemplified by data
like *un espèce de cochon* 'a real pig; lit. a sort of pig' in French. Jones (1996,
222; see also Grevisse 1986, §303) notes that expressions like these often
convey a derogatory attitude toward the person or thing, which is due to
the choice of epithet noun. Other examples include *ce putain de livre* 'this
bloody book' (note this use of *putain* is quite European; Laurentian French
would have *ce crisse de livre*), *un imbécile de professeur* 'this imbecile of a professor', along with a few instances of nonpejorative usage such as *un ange
d'enfant* 'an angel of a child'.[8] Grevisse cites as well examples with *drôle de*, as
in *une drôle de nation* 'a crazy nation', and *une diable de*, as in *une diable d'idée*
'a devil of an idea'. All of these examples are rather hyperbolic in connota-
tion, and in this sense borrowed *quite* fits in well with them.

Jones notes that *un espèce de cochon*-type constructions have a very particular form of gender agreement: for example, *espèce* 'species' is feminine
and would take *une* as the correct form of the indefinite article, whereas
this particular construction has the gender of the final noun (e.g., *un espèce
de cochon* where *cochon* is masculine).[9] Making the link between *un espèce de
cochon* and *un vrai cochon* 'a real pig', where *vrai* is an adjective, Jones suggests that *espèce*, like *vrai*, modifies the head noun, *cochon*. Such an analysis
fits with the data in (16), *un quite de bon souper*, since it is *souper* that takes
adjectival modification (as in the common European French expression *un
espèce de petit con* 'a real bastard; lit. a sort of little bastard'. Since *souper*, like
*cochon*, is the head, masculine gender on the article is accounted for, as is
feminine gender in (12), *une quite de visite*, since *visite* is feminine.

What is left to account for is the presence of *de*: Jones suggests that
*espèce* and other nouns occupying the same position bear the abstract case
feature assigned to the NP (or, DP, in more current treatments), "usurp-

ing" the case assigned to the whole phrase. Thus, they pattern like quantity nouns, as does *douzaine* in *une douzaine de pommes* 'lit. a dozen of apples'. Following this line of argumentation, the preposition *de* must appear to assign case to the head noun.

We are now led to consider the grammatical category of *quite*. It is clearly not an adverb in (12)–(14) nor is it one in (16). Is it a modifying noun, on the model of the French-origin modifiers we have seen thus far? Along with data that clearly involve noun modifiers, there are also cases like *une drôle d'histoire* 'a really funny story', where *drôle* might be regarded as an adjective (this example is noted by Grevisse but not by Jones in this regard).[10] However, it is possible to use *drôle* in its canonical postnominal adjective slot, as in *une histoire drôle* 'a funny story' as well. *Quite* does not enter into such an alternation nor can it be modified, as we have seen. In fact, it seems most closely related to expressions of quantity, as in *une douzaine de pommes*, noted above, or *beaucoup de vin* 'a lot of wine', where the *de* phrase contains the head noun.[11] In this regard, it is noteworthy that clitization of [*de* PRONOUN] as *en* is possible, indeed required, with the Acadian *quite* construction (18) and with these expressions of quantity (19).

18. *Il   en    a          acheté   une   douzaine.*
    he   some  have.3SG.PRES  bought   a     dozen
    'He bought a dozen of them'

19. *Il   en              contait   une   quite.*
    he   some  have.3SG.PRES  told     a     quite
    'He told quite a one'

However, whereas native speaker judgments accept structure like (20), structures like (21) are vastly preferred.

20. *J'    en    ai          rêvé      un   drôle.*
    1PERS  some  have.1SG.PRES  dreamed   a    strange
    'I dreamed a strange one'

21. *J'    en    ai          rêvé    un   qui    était       drôle.*
    1PERS  some  have.1SG.PRES  dreamed  one  which  be.3SG.IMP  strange
    'I dreamed one which was strange'

*En* cliticization with other members of the *espèce de cochon* set is uniformly judged to be ungrammatical.[12]

22. *\*Il   en    est            un   espèce.*
    he   some  be.1SG.PRES     a    sort
    'He is a sort of one'

We may conclude, then, that Baie Sainte-Marie Acadian *quite* patterns semantically with the English peripheral modifier but syntactically with French quantity expressions.

The student of English historical linguistics will probably be aware of the fact that peripheral focus modifiers are a relevantly recent phenomenon in Germanic: Stoffel (1901; cited by Traugott 2006, 335) notes that *quite* was borrowed into Middle English from French and is ultimately of Latin origin (*quietus* 'clean, free'), although it must be said that the *Oxford English Dictionary* does give some earlier attestations. Stoffel says that until the eighteenth century *quite* was used exclusively in collocations like *quite clean*: he cites an 1862 edition of the British satirical magazine *Punch*, which characterizes its use in expressions like *quite a number* as 'ridiculous'.

On first encounter, the *quite* construction seems strange to the nonnative speaker of this Acadian variety. On closer inspection, we see that what is a highly restricted phenomenon in English has been pulled into line with the syntax of French. We have seen, then, that English provides an important resource for the generation of new intensifiers in contemporary Acadian French varieties spoken in language contact situations. Where such intensifiers occur in English collocations that are at odds with the syntax of French, they are syntactically incorporated into the host grammar.

## BORROWED DISCOURSE MARKERS

The topic of borrowed discourse markers is not a new one in the literature on North American French. Mougeon and Hébrard (1975) report that English *anyway, well, you know,* and the like are associated with the working-class French of Welland, Ontario, in particular with speakers who speak both French and English on a regular basis. Roy's (1979) study of Moncton French focused in part on borrowed discourse markers, such as *well* and *but*, illlustrated in (23) and (24), respectively:

23. *I    vivent    su    la    terre,    pi    de    temps en temps,    well*
    they  live-3PL.PRES  on  the  earth  and  from  time  in  time  well
    *i    vont    travailler...*
    they  go.3PL.PRES  work-INF
    'The live on earth and from time to time, well, they go to work...'

24. *Je    veux    back    aller    à    l'    école    parce...    toutes*
    1PERS  want.SG.PRES  back  go-INF  to  the  school  because  all
    *mes    amis    sont    là    but...*
    my  friends  be.3PL.PRES  there  but
    '...I want to go back to school because ... all my friends are there but...'

Borrowed discourse markers have also been investigated for this variety by Chevalier (2002) and Petraş (2005), among others. The discourse markers given above are found in all of the contact varieties of Acadian French (King 2008) and in Louisiana French (Picone 1993; Rottet 2001).

In considering single-word code-switches and borrowings, it is important to keep in mind that filling a lexical gap in the host language is only one of many motivations for language mixture. For instance, Moncton French has French-origin equivalents to discursive *so* (*ça fait que*) and *but* (*mais*), while *well* has a number of French equivalents depending on the context. One goal of code-switching and borrowing research is determining the social and discursive conditions under which other-language material comes to serve as *le mot juste*. Given sufficient intensity of contact, words like *but*, which may be used as a conjunction in English as well as a discourse marker, may take on this function in the borrowing language as well. This is the case in Moncton French, although Roy (1979) notes that some of her consultants appeared to actively resist extension to the grammatical domain. This does not appear to be the case in Prince Edward Island, where we encounter clear conjunctive uses of *but*, as in (25), taken from the Saint-Louis corpus, as well as discursive *but*:

25. *Ça coute      plus  à  vivre,  but  le  monde  fait          de*
    it  cost.SG.PRES more to live-INF but the people make.SG.PRES of
    *la    belle · argent*
    the good  money
    'It costs more to live but people make good money'

However, while it is the case that where we find, say, conjunctive use of particular lexical items, we will also find them used as discourse markers, the reverse is not true. It seems, then, that borrowings may often begin life in usage which is fairly peripheral to the grammar but, under the right social conditions, go on to play a more grammatical role. Based on frequency and distribution in their respective corpora, Roy (1979) and Mougeon and Beniak (1991) assign to the English discourse markers the status of borrowing (versus code-switch). Mougeon and Beniak put forth the following hypothesis as to why we might find borrowed discourse markers:

[T]hat sentence connectors and other kinds of discourse organizers like *so* are so often reported in lists of core lexical borrowings may not be a coincidence, since these items all occur at prime [code]switch points. We would tentatively advance the hypothesis that core lexical borrowings like *so* and other sentence connectors may start out as codeswitches (either as single words or as part of switched sentences) which by dint of repetition become loanwords. [211]

Another case in point is English *whatever*, ubiquitous in Acadian varieties spoken in contact with English. In (26) and (27), I give examples from southeastern New Brunswick (Turpin 1998) and from Prince Edward Island (King 2000), respectively.

26. *Ça a*         *fait un façon de noise, j'*    *ai*
    it have.3SG.PRES    a    sort of noise 1PERS have.1SG.PRES
    *hallé*    *la*    *clutch, pullé over, j'*    *ai*       *dit* «*Whatever.*»
    hauled the clutch pulled over 1PERS have.1SG.PRES said whatever
    'It made a sort of noise, I hauled in the clutch, pulled over, I said, "Whatever"'
27. *On*   *sautait*     *de*    *la*    *corde ou whatever.*
    one jump-SG.IMP PART the rope or whatever
    'We used to skip rope or whatever'

Notice that in (26), it is not clear from the single example whether *whatever* is a code-switch or a borrowing, whereas in (27) it is part of a code-swich, *ou whatever*. Along with usage as in (26) and (27), we also find usage as in (28) and (29) from the Prince Edward Island corpus (King 1991, 2000), (30) and (31) from the Grosses Coques, Nova Scotia, corpus, and (32) and (33) from southeastern New Brunswick (Perrot 1995).

28. *Je*    *m'en vas*      *l'*    *acheter*    *whatever quoi ce-qu' elle*
    1PERS REFL go.SG.PRES her buy-INF whatever what that she
    *veut*         *pour Noël.*
    wants.SG.PRES for Christmas
    'I am going to buy her whatever she wants for Christmas'
29. *Il*   *courait*     *wherever*   *que ç' a*        *arrêté.*
    he run-SG.IMP wherever that it have.SG.PRES stopped
    'He ran wherever it came to rest'
30. *C' est*        *un fusil avec un scope, whatever que c' est.*
    it be.3SG.PRES a gun with a scope whatever that it be.3SG.PRES
    'It's a gun with a scope, whatever that is'
31. *Il*   *voulait*     *parler*    *à*    *whoever qu' il y*     *avait*
    he want.SG.IMP speak-INF to whoever that it there have.SG.IMP
    *su*   *le*    *telephone.*
    on the telephone
    'He wanted to speak to whoever was on the telephone'
32. *whoever qui travaille*     *à*    *McDonald's*
    whoever who work.SG.PRES at McDonald's
    'whoever works at McDonald's'
33. *whenever je watch*       *ça*
    whenever I watch.SG.PRES that
    'whenever I watch that'

The *wh-ever* words in (28)–(32) all involve free relative clauses, which carry an indefinite reading. In Standard French, these meanings would be rendered by expressions such as *n'importe* (e.g., *n'importe qui* 'anybody') or *peu importe* (e.g., *peu importe qui* 'no matter who') or the *wh-*word plus *que* (e.g., *quoi que ça soit* 'lit. what that it be'). However, *quoi que* and the like are unavailable for such use in Acadian French because moved *wh-*words always co-occur with the complementizer and as such always carry a definite reading (e.g., *Quoi ce-qu'il a fait?* 'What did he do?'). While an indefinite reading can be obtained in Acadian varieties through the use of *n'importe où*, *n'importe quand*, and the like, it should be noted that French is much less consistent than English in how such a reading is achieved, since the latter makes use of *wh-ever* words (*whatever, wherever, whoever, however, whenever*, etc.). As I have shown elsewhere (King 2000), the Prince Edward Island varieties allow structures both with and without a French-origin *wh-*phrase along with English-origin *wh-ever*, so we might schematize free relatives in that variety linearly as involving the sequence *Xever (X ce) que....* At first glance, it would seem that the *wh-ever* word serves as a modifier in (28). However, if this were the case, one should not expect the French *wh-*word to be optional; we would not expect to find *whatever que*, as in (28). So the *wh-ever* words must be "real" *wh-*words.[13]

Looking across a number of Acadian French varieties, it now appears that free relatives of the *whatever quoi ce-que*–type are a transitional stage on the way to "bare" *wh-ever que*–type free relatives. Only the latter are found in the Grosses Coques corpus, for instance, or are cited by Flikeid (1989a) for other Nova Scotia varieties. On the other hand, the L'Anse-à-Canards, Newfoundland, variety has *whatever* only as a discourse marker, as in (23) and (24). Perrot's (1995) data for southeastern New Brunswick shows *wh-ever + que*, as in (31), and *wh-ever* on its own as in (32). However, it is important to keep in mind that Perrot's data come from adolescent speakers for whom it is not clear that they (necessarily) have Doubly-filled Comp, as do traditional Acadian varieties. We lack data from older speakers for this and quite a number of other variables for present-day southeastern New Brunswick speakers. We do know that what ends up as a rearrangement of the free relative system begins life with discursive *whatever*. Roy (1979) gives us some time depth, since, in her study of the Moncton French, she does not report borrowed interrogative pronouns of the *wh-ever*-type found in subsequent studies of adolescent southeastern New Brunswick speech based on corpora constructed in the 1990s.

## CODE-SWITCHING AND THE EXPRESSION
## OF EVIDENTIALITY

I conclude this section by turning to one final set of discourse markers, which includes the fairly ubiquitous code-switch, *I guess,* also found at the edge of utterances, as in (33), taken from the Abram-Village, Prince Edward Island, corpus.

> 33. *Il a marié la deuxième femme, I guess.*
>     he have.3SG.PRES married the second wife I guess
>     'He married the second wife, I guess'

There is another use of *I guess* in these two corpora, one in which English provides the matrix verb along with a first-person singular pronominal subject, as in (34), taken from King and Nadasdi's (1999) study of French-English code-switching. This example comes from Abram-Village, while the one in (35) comes from the Grosses Coques, Nova Scotia, corpus.

> 34. *I guess qu' on est pas mal tout pareil.*
>     I guess that one be.3SG.PRES NEG bad all alike
>     'I guess that we are just about all equal'
> 35. *I guess qu' il s' a emprunté de l' argent.*
>     I guess that he REFL have.3SG.PRES borrowed of the money
>     'I guess that he borrowed himself some money'

King and Nadasdi (1999) found that *I guess* is the most frequent of a particular class of evidentials, verbs of opinion or belief, used in this way in the Prince Edward Island varieties. While a number of individual verbs are involved, the subject of the matrix clause is always in the first-person singular. In the Saint-Louis corpus, matrix clause *I guess* actually outstrips quantitatively its use as a discourse marker. Even in varieties with less contact with English, such as the Newfoundland varieties, one finds discursive *I guess* and "grammatical" *I guess.* Table 6.1, adapted from King and Nadasdi (1999), compares use of English code-switches involving evidential verbs in a three-community corpus. In the Newfoundland variety, English code-switching does not extend to other evidential verbs as it does in Prince Edward Island Acadian and, from what we can see from the literature, in southeastern New Brunswick Acadian.

King and Nadasdi (1999) argue that English matrix clauses involving first-person use of evidential verbs serve to underscore a speaker's opinion relative to the veracity of the event. We suggest that the degree of uncertainty that accompanies switching to *I guess* has since become associated with all semantically related code-switches to English, particularly in the

TABLE 6.1

Distribution of Evidential Verbs Used in English Code-Switches
by Community and Linguistic Environment

| Verb | Saint-Louis, P.E.I. | | Abram-Village, P.E.I. | | L'Anse-à-Canards, N.L. | |
|---|---|---|---|---|---|---|
| | *Matrix* | *Elsewhere* | *Matrix* | *Elsewhere* | *Matrix* | *Elsewhere* |
| *am sure* | 3 | 0 | 1 | 0 | 0 | 0 |
| *believe* | 4 | 2 | 2 | 2 | 0 | 0 |
| *bet* | 2 | 2 | 0 | 0 | 0 | 0 |
| *can't see* | 1 | 0 | 0 | 0 | 0 | 0 |
| *doubt* | 0 | 0 | 0 | 1 | 0 | 0 |
| *guess* | 98 | 85 | 23 | 97 | 17 | 69 |
| *imagine* | 8 | 8 | 0 | 0 | 0 | 0 |
| *know* (*don't know*) | 1 (0) | 3 (47) | 0 | 2 (4) | 0 | 0 |
| *suppose* | 0 | 6 | 0 | 0 | 0 | 0 |
| *think* (*don't think*) | 43 (4) | 47 (19) | 0 | 5 (3) | 0 | 0 |

case of the heavy code-switchers, who are at the vanguard of such usage. The example in (36) comes from Perrot's (1995) study of southeastern New Brunswick adolescent usage, while the example in (37) comes from Saint-Louis.

36. *I hope    que    mon   père      a                       callé    ma    mère.*
    I hope   that   my    father   have.3SG.PRES   called   my    mother
    'I hope that my father called my mother'

37. *I think    j'       ai                       plus   peur   des     chenilles     qu'    une*
    I think   1PERS   have.1SG.PRES   more   fear   some   caterpillars   than   a
    *serpent.*
    snake
    'I think I'm more afraid of caterpillars than a snake'

The story does not end here, however. The evidential study led to an investigation of variable presence/absence of the complementizer *que* in the Saint-Louis variety, the community that proved most advanced with respect to using English code-switches. King and Nadasdi (2006) found that, as in prior studies of other varieties (e.g., Sankoff 1980 for Montreal French; Martineau 1988 and Dion 2003 for Ottawa-Hull French), following phonological environment was found to play an important role in constraining variation. Presence/absence of the *que* complementizer is predictable in part in terms of the Sonority Hierarchy: *que* absence is least frequent before a following vowel, more frequent before a following sonorant and most frequent before a following obstruent. Proportion of *que* absence with first-person singular tokens was quite high for evidential use of French-origin verbs like *croire* (79%), *penser* (88%), *savoir* (65%), and *trouver* (98%).[14] *Je crois, je pense, je trouve,* and the like are considered parentheticals in the discourse literature: they modify or weaken the claim to the truth of the proposition. In the examples contained in (38) and (39), the main assertion is contained in the subordinate clause.

38. *C' est        ça, je     pense.*
    it be.3SG.PRES    1PERS think.SG.PRES
    'That's it, I think'

39. *Ils    venont      de soir,    je     crois       bien.*
    they come.3PL.PRES of evening 1PERS believe.SG.PRES well
    'They are coming this evening, I believe'

As matrix clauses, such parentheticals have been argued to provide the "weak link" that allows *que* absence (Warren 1994). While the semantics of the verb provides a partial account of the French language data, it fails to account for data involving corresponding English matrix verbs in the Saint-Louis corpus, where *que* is almost invariably present for the data presented in table 6.1. In fact, there are only three cases of *que* absence with English evidentials. The facts are thus the mirror image of one another, depending on the language of the matrix clause: with English matrix verbs, the effects of verb semantics are overridden by a strong tendency to syntactically integrate the "other language" material into French discourse.

## CONCLUSION

The reader will have noticed that I have refrained from discussing English-origin phenomena until the final quarter of the book, in part because of the way Acadian varieties are often negatively stereotyped in this regard. While professional audiences may not jump to the conclusion that these varieties are going to hell in a handbasket, some members of such audiences have not been immune to snickering at some of the sample sentences I have presented here. However, with the background presented in earlier chapters regarding the conservative nature of some of these varieties for a number of grammatical variables, the innovations described in these chapters are now well contextualized. Acadian French is both conservative and innovative, which is what we would expect from varieties with low degrees of normative pressure. We have seen in this chapter and in the previous one that, while English-influenced innovations are several, they are constrained by the host grammar.

# 7. CONCLUSION

In part, this book has described a journey undertaken in the late nineteenth century by the enterprising American graduate student James Geddes in Baie-des-Chaleurs, New Brunswick and by early folklorists and linguists like Pascal Poirier in New Brunswick, and Alcée Fortier in Louisiana. By the mid-twentieth century, the Quebec folklorist Luc Lacourcière had made an invaluable set of recordings in New Brunswick and Prince Edward Island. An amazing number of Louisiana State University graduate students had worked on the Louisiana varieties since the 1930s, with John Guilbeau completing a Ph.D. on the Lafourche dialect in 1952 at the University of North Carolina. By that time, Geneviève Massignon was working on her massive lexical study of Maritime Acadian varieties, which would be published in 1962. Following quickly upon Guilbeau, John Garner completed his Ph.D. dissertation on comparative Acadian French phonology in 1952 at the University of Texas.

In 1986 the Nova Scotia linguist B. Edward Gesner would justifiably state that there were very few works on the Atlantic Canada Acadian varieties prior to 1960 and go on to document what he viewed to be an astonishing surge of interest in Acadian language and culture over the next 25 years in his *Bibliographie annotée de linguistique acadienne*. Gesner (1986, 1) marvels that "between 1980 and 1985, in the space of just five years, more than 75 studies of Acadian linguistics have been completed and several research projects, some of them large scale, [were] in progress" (my translation).[1] This explosion of interest has not lagged, as even a cursory view of the bibliography and contents of the present work will show. Since Gesner's bibliography was published, a large body of sociolinguistic literature, as well as more traditional dialectological and some formal works, have appeared. Our knowledge of Acadian French and related varieties had become such that, by the turn of the twenty-first century, large-scale comparative work of the type undertaken here could be conducted.

In this book I have focused on analyzing data drawn from face-to-face interaction and, to a lesser degree, from written sources. I have also discussed in considerable detail the language use of residents of particular Atlantic Canada communities, such as L'Anse-à-Canards, Newfoundland; Grosses-Coques, Nova Scotia; Abram-Village, Prince Edward Island; and Moncton, New Brunswick. I have drawn on the extant literature and primary data sources available to me for other Atlantic Canada communities and for Louisiana. In explaining the structure of large and small data sets and their relevance for a comparative sociolinguistics of Acadian French, I have tried as well to convey why these varieties remain as exciting to me as they did many years ago when I did my first fieldwork in L'Anse-à-Canards, Newfoundland, research that culminated in my 1978 M.A. thesis.

Acadian French has much to offer the student of French linguistics and of linguistics generally: it is terrain marked by old rivalries (e.g., the simple past versus the present perfect), new players (e.g., intensifiers), theoretical puzzles (e.g., the mechanics of subject-verb agreement), and, it should go without saying, at times recalcitrant data. I have tried to exemplify all of this here.

Future research on these varieties can profitably go in a number of directions. We need more data for some of these varieties, like southeastern New Brunswick, where a modern sociolinguistic corpus for a wide age range would be particularly useful. We also look forward to more research results for the Îles de la Madeleine variety, spoken in a setting which has historically combined both isolation from other French varieties AND from English. However, it must also be kept in mind that the socioeconomic situation of the early twenty-first century has seen a collapse of traditional industry, a turn to (inter)national tourism as an important new income source, and a large expatriate Acadian community forced to leave their homes for higher-paying work in richer provinces. The study of Acadian French, then, needs to go beyond its traditional territorial boundaries. Further, the use of Acadian French in mediated contexts—in comic books, in television series (such as *Acadieman*), in Facebook groups, in YouTube videos, in personal blogs, and in new music—also provide data for study. Such data will need the careful methodological considerations that I have urged here with regard to older data sources that involve stylized performance, as well as new theorizing about Acadian-ness and what constitutes Acadian French. The future of studies of these varieties thus seems quite promising.

# APPENDIX: SAMPLE NARRATIVES OF PERSONAL EXPERIENCE, GROSSES COQUES, NOVA SCOTIA

## NARRATIVE 1

OR: Il y en avait (IMP) un autre … une femme qu'avait venu (PP) là et il y avait (IMP) deux enfants.
['There is another one … a woman had come and there were two children.']

OR: Il y en un qu'avait (IMP) about deux ans de vieux, l'autre trois ou quatre.
['There was one about two years old, the other three or four.']

OR: Puis c'était (IMP) dans le mois de mars.
['And it was in the month of March.']

OR: Il faisait (IMP) une frette.
['It was a cold (day).']

OR: C'était (IMP) une journée entoure de zéro.
['It was around zero degrees.']

OR: J'avais (IMP) un vieux bot là, tu te souviens (PRES) peut-être de ce bot-là? (Oui. Oui.)
['I had an old boat, you perhaps remember that old boat? (Yes, yes.)']

OR: Il y avait (IMP) de l'eau dedans.
['There was water in (it).']

OR: Il y avait (IMP) about ça d'eau dedans.
['There was about that much water in (it).']

OR: Puis il y avait (IMP) de la glace about ça puis ils avient cassé (IMP) la glace.
['And there was ice around and they broke through the ice.']

OR: Ils s'avient déshabillés (PP) nu cul
['They had gotten undressed, bare naked.']

CA: et puis le plus petit, le plus vieux là, grimpit (SP) le plus petit
['and the littlest one, the oldest one, climbed on the littlest']

CA: puis il le poussit (SP) en haut.
['and pushed him up']

OR: Ça faisait (IMP) about haut de même pour embarquer.
['It was about that high to get on board.']

CA: Puis là, le plus petit grimpit (SP) l'autre
['Then the littlest one grabbed the other.']

CA: puis il le hallit (SP) en dedans par les bras
['and he halled him in by the arms']

OR: puis ils étiont (IMP) dans l'eau
['then they were in the water (i.e. in the bottom of the boat)']

OR: puis ils s'en-, ils s'enjoyiont (IMP)
['and they were enjoying themselves']

CA: puis je vus (SP) ça à la vitre.
['and I saw that from the window.']

CA: Je fus (SP) là.
['I went there.']

CA: Je dis (SP? PRES?) "Il y a une femme qu'a, qu'a deux enfants icitte là."
['I say? said?, "There is a woman who has who has two children out there."']

CA: Je dis (SP? PRES?), "Je sais (PRES) point si c'est des Eskimos ou quoi ce-que c'est
   (PRES) mais j'aimerais qu'elle sortit, qu'elle vient (PRES) icitte me, me parler."
['I say? said?, "I don't know if they are Eskimos or whatever it is but I would like
   her to leave, that she come here to speak to me."']

CA: Ça fait qu'elle arrivit (SP).
['So she arrived.']

CA: Elle dit (SP? PRES?) "Quoi ce-qu'ils ont fait asteure?"
['She says? said?, "What are they doing this time?"']

CA: Bien, je dis (SP? PRES?) "Viens (IMPER) voir."
['I say? said?, "Come and see."']

CA: Quand ce-qu'elle vut (SP) ça,
['When she saw that,']

CA: "Oh," elle dit (SP? PRES?), "mes petits son of a gun."
['"Oh," she says? said?, "my little son of a guns!"']

CA: Elle grimpit (SP) ça
['She grabbed them']

CA: puis elle fourrit (SP) ça dans la |car.
['and she stuffed them in the car.']

CA: Elle dit (SP? PRES?) "Vous habillerez!"
['She says? said?, "Get dressed!"']

OR: Elle était (IMP) rien que rentrée qu'ils étiont (IMP) retourné back dans l'eau.
['She had only just come back in when they were back in the water again.']

CA: Puis là, le monde se commencit (SP) à se havrer à la vitre puis voir, sortir dehors.
['And the, people started to gather at the window and look, to go outside.']

OR: Il y en avait (IMP) peut-être une dizaine, quinzaine là en toute.
['There were perhaps ten, fifteen there in all.']

CA: Elle grimpit (SP) ça par le chignon du cou, par les cheveux, un bras su l'autre.
['She grabbed them by the scruff of the neck, by the hair, one in each arm.']

CA: Elle dit (SP? PRES?) "Dans la sacrée car!"
['She says? said?, "In the bloody car!"']

CA: Elle dit (SP? PRES?) "C'est là où ce-que vous allez aller!"
['She says? said?, "That's where you are going to go!"']

CA: Puis elle fut (SP) rentrée puis elle fut (SP) chercher l'autre.
['Then she went back to get the other one.']

CA: Elle dit (SP? PRES?), "Vous en, tu t'en viendras."
  ['She says? said?, "You, you come here."']
CA: Elle dit (SP? PRES?), "Je vas les mener (PF) chus nous."
  ['She says? said?, "I am going to take them home!"']

## NARRATIVE 2

OR: [C'était] il y a (PRES) trois ans de cecitte. Moi, là, faut que je me mette (PRES. SUBJ) loin.
  ['It was three years ago. I've got to go back a ways.']
  (Oh, oui.)
  (Oh, yes.)
OR: Moi, j'avais jamais tiré (PP) du fusil avant.
  ['Me, I had never fired a gun before.']
OR: Bien jamais, parce je sais (PRES) point.
  ['Well never, because I don't know how.']
OR: J'en avions (IMP) point su mon père.
  ['We didn't have any at my father's.']
OR: Anyway, je furent (SP) à la |camp, moi et N***,
  ['Anyway, we were at the camp, me and N***']
OR: puis lui, il garochait (IMP) après les goélands.
  ['and him, he was shooting at seagulls.']
OR: Ça fait (PRES), "Pow, pow, pow, pow, pow."
  ['It goes, "Pow, pow, pow, pow."']
CA: Il dit, "Faut (PRES) que t'apprennes (PRES.SUBJ) à garocher du fusil."
  ['He says? said?, "You need to learn to shoot a gun."']
OR: puis c'est (PRES) un fusil avec un scope, whatever que c'est (PRES).
  ['And it's a gun with a scope, whatever that is.']
CA: So il mit (SP) un petit bois.
  ['So he put out a little stick.']
CA: Il plantit (SP) un bois,
  ['He stuck a stick in the ground']
OR: puis il était (IMP) comme, moi, j'étais (IMP) su la pavé puis lui était (IMP) au lac
  ['and he was like, me, I was on the ground and he was by the lake']
OR: puis il faisait (IMP) de planter le bois
  ['and he was sticking the stick in the ground']
CA: so moi, je pris (SP) le fusil.
  ['so I took the gun']
CA: Je dis, "Norman, je te vois (PRES) dans l'X."
  ['I say? said?, "Norman, I see you in the X."']
OR: J'oubli-, bien je le voyais (IMP).
  ['I forget-, well, I saw him']

CA: Il dit, "God damn! Tu mettras (FUT) ce fusil-là su le pavé puis je veux (PRES) jamais back."

['He says? said, "God damn! You put that gun on the ground and I never want [to see you with it] again."']

EV: Mais je le voyais (IMP).

['But I saw him.']

EV: Mais je le vois (PRES) encore, il plantait (IMP) le petit bois,

['But I (can) still see him, he was sticking the little stick in the ground']

CA: je huchis (SP), "N***!"

['I cried out, "N***!"']

OR: Mais c'est (PRES) comme ça je le fis (SP),

['but it's like that (that) I did it']

CA: Je dis, "Je te vois (PRES) dans l'X."

['I say? said?, "I see you in the X."']

CO/EV: Il manquit (SP) de me tuer.

['He almost killed me.']

(Toi, tu manquis de le tuer, lui.)

['You, you almost killed him.']

OR: Mais oui. Oui, mais j'allais (IMP) pas haler.

['Yes, of course. Yes, but I wasn't going to pull the trigger.']

CA: Il dit, "Tu mettras (FUT) le fusil su la, la table."

['He says? said?, "(You) put the gun on the, the table."']

OR: À ce temps-là, c'était (IMP) la table su le pavé.

['At the time, there was the table on the patio.']

CA: puis il dit, "Je veux jamais que tu touches un fusil back. Point les miens."

['and he says? said?, "I never want you to touch a gun again. Not mine."']

CO/EV: Mais il m'a jamais pardonné (PRESPERF) pour.

['But he never forgave me for (it).']


## NARRATIVE 3

OR: C'était (IMP) un samedi au soir.

['It was Saturday night.']

OR: N*** et J*** étiont (IMP) partis mettre de l'air dans leur tank.

['N*** and J*** were gone to put air in their tank.']

OR: Je voulais (IMP) point aller avec eux.

['I didn't want to go with them.']

Je dis, "Je vas aller (PF) me quérir des poires au Farmers' Market puis je vas les bouteiller (PF) en guêttant que vous arriviez (PRES.SUBJ) back."

['I say? said? "I'm going to get some pears at the Farmers' Market and then I'm going to bottle them while I wait for you to come back."']

OR: Il était (IMP) vers huit heures.

['It was around eight o'clock.']

CA: Je rentris (IMP) dans le logis.

['I went back to the house.']

CA: Je mis (SP) la light.

['I turned on the light.']

OR: Mais ça me semblait (IMP) qu'il y avait (IMP) de quoi de noir qu'avait passé.

['But it seemed to me that there was something dark that went by.']

CA: God damn! Je mis (SP) d'autres lights.

['God damn! I turned on some other lights.']

CA: Je mis (SP) la light là.

['I turned on the light over there.']

CA: Je m'assis (SP) là.

['I sat down.']

OR: Il y avait (IMP) de quoi qui flyait (IMP) dessous le beam.

['There was something that flew under the beam.']

OR: Puis ça prenait (IMP) par là.

['It was right over there.']

CA: Je dis, "Une souris chauve!"

['I say? said? "A bat!"']

CA: Je pris (SP) pour ma chamber et je fermis (SP) la porte.

['I took off for my bedroom and I shut the door.']

CA: Je callis (SP) B***, le père à N***.

['I called B***, N***'s father.']

CA: Je dis, "Faut (PRES) que tu viennes (PRES.SUBJ) icitte!"

['I say? said? "You've got to come over here!"']

CA: Je dis, "Il y a (PRES) une souris chauve dans le logis!"

['I say? said? "There's a bat in the house!"']

CA: Mais il dit, "Prend (IMPER) la balai et tue-la (IMPER)!"

['So he says? said? "Take a broom and kill it!"']

CA: Je dis, "Quoi-ce tu crois que je te calle (PRES) pour? Viens (IMPER) vite!"

['I say? said? "What do you think I called you for? Come quick!"']

OR: Puis lui croit (PRES) que c'est (PRES) une joke!

['But he thinks it's a joke!']

CA: So il l'attrapée (PRESPERF).

['So he caught it.']

(Bien c'est point une joke.)

['(Well, that's not a joke.)']

CO/EV: C'est (PRES) point une joke.

['It's not a joke.']

CO/EV: God damn de fucking souris chauve qui flyait (IMP)!

['God damn fucking bat flying around!']

CO/EV: C'est (PRES) que … ils disont (PRES) que ça va (PRES) dans tes cheveux mais… ça flyait (IMP)!

['It's that… they say that it gets in your hair but…it was flying around!']

CO/EV: Et il l'a attrapée (PRESPERF), elle était (IMP) point morte!

['And he caught it, it wasn't dead!']

# NOTES

## CHAPTER 1

1. This chapter has benefited greatly from the works of Arsenault (1987), Griffiths (1992), Ross and Deveau (1992), and Butler (1995).

2. See Daigle (1980) for more detail on French-English conflicts during this period.

3. While France lost control of the then-uninhabited islands of Saint-Pierre and Miquelon, the British claim was relinquished under the Treaty of Paris in 1763. From that point on, the islands would be the last French territory in North America.

4. Throughout most of the history of French language education in Acadia, and in Canada more generally, Standard Metropolitan French has been the norm or target. The idea that educated Quebec French should be taught in Canadian classrooms dates only from the 1970s, first endorsed by the Assemblée générale de l'Association québécoise des professeurs de français and at the time viewed as a revolutionary idea (Maurais 1993). The success of this move toward use of the regional standard is evidenced in the 1990s by the fact that Canadian-published French first-language dictionaries no longer flag Quebec French vocabulary as regionalisms.

5. The literature on Acadian French tends to use *Pubnico* as a cover term for the Argyle area, which includes the town of Pubnico, along with the communities of Sainte Anne du Ruisseau, Tusket, Wedgeport, Butte Amirault, etc.

6. I use the term *Standard French* throughout this work to refer to the superposed layer of linguistic knowledge taught in schools and throughout the francophone world. When this idealization is subject to regional differences relevant to the discussion, for example, where normative Quebec French differs from its Metropolitan counterpart, more specific terminology is used. See Milroy and Milroy (1987) for discussion of language prescription and standardization and Valdman (1979) on the choice of appropriate terminology in work on French. While the term *français de référence* is becoming more and more accepted in French, its English equivalent, *Referential French*, is not well known.

7. Interestingly, at the time my Prince Edward Island corpus was constructed, the late 1980s, it was science and mathematics that were taught in English, a matter of some debate among community residents.

8. The three Maritime Provinces, along with the province of Newfoundland and Labrador, constitute Canada's Atlantic Provinces. The vast majority of residents of Newfoundland and Labrador live on the island of Newfoundland. Since mainland Labrador is not relevant for Acadian settlement, its history is not discussed in the present work.

9.  A few octagenarians I interviewed in 1980 could recall fragments of Breton prayers and songs learned from their Breton fathers and in one case an additional half dozen core vocabulary items.

10.  "[L]a cohésion interne de la communauté et l'emploi très élevé du français dans la plupart des domaines de communication sont exceptionnelles parmi les régions francophones en dehors du Quebec."

11.  The southwest region of New Brunswick has a very small francophone population, but it has not to my knowledge been the object of linguistic research.

12.  Data for ethnic origin are recorded in the census as "single origin" (with British, French, or "other" specified) or as simply "multiple origins." While it is tempting to infer that those who give "multiple origins" are (partly) of French descent (raising the figures for French ethnic origin given in the text), I have not done so, as there is no independent means of establishing this fact. Exclusion of "multiple origins" responses thus may skew the picture somewhat.

13.  The fact that more people claim to speak French as their mother tongue and as their home language than say they are of French origin is probably explained by the fact that the ethnic origin question allows the option of choosing "multiple origins."

14.  This figure of 3,000 is given in Thomas (1983, 50). Two trends tend to make it difficult to determine the actual number of francophones in western Newfoundland: a tendency to underreport French usage in government census up to at least the 1970s due to lack of prestige of the local variety and an opposite tendency to overreport the number of people who still speak French on the part of enthusiastic "preservers" of French language and culture. My own figures are based on house-by-house surveys conducted with the assistance of community residents in the late 1970s and early 1980s in the five communities commonly accepted to have at least several French speakers. These figures are in line with those cited by Butler (1990).

15.  Unfortunately, at the time of writing, very little linguistic research had been published on this variety, although it should be noted that a major sociolinguistic survey is currently underway, under the direction of Carmen LeBlanc.

## CHAPTER 2

1.  Following current practice, I use *Laurentian French* as a cover term for those varieties of French that owe their origins to the settlement of New France on the banks of the St. Lawrence River. It includes, along with Quebec French, Ontario French and western Canadian varieties that resulted from nineteenth-century migration from Quebec.

2.  Note that while we are able to analyze nineteenth-century theatrical representations of Quebec French, there is no Acadian theatre before the twentieth century.

3. "[E]n sa qualité de document transmis de bouche à oreille d'une génération à l'autre, [le conte] reproduit avant tout la langue du passé.... Il reflète la langue orale dans son usage le plus littéraire" (Péronnet 1995, 39).

4. This folktale is known as Hansel and Gretal in Germanic, including English, tradition. I follow folkloristic convention and cite the folktale according to the Aarne/Thompson (1961) classification scheme.

5. Since Geddes does not mention use of "traditional" Acadian variants such as first-person plural *je*, we may assume that this variety was even then less conservative than some present-day Acadian varieties.

6. In the course of its history, French grammaticized several formerly positive expressions as negators, including *pas* 'step', *point* 'point', *mie* 'crumb', and *goutte* 'drop' (Jesperson 1917). In most varieties, however, *pas* is the general negator and *point* is now a stylistic variant, typically linked to emphasis. To my knowledge, *mie* and *goutte* are no longer attested as negators in French.

7. A few other French Newfoundlanders were recorded by Peacock, but over half of the 40 French-language recordings were made of Madame LeCostard. Note that this consultant's surname is variously spelled *LeCostard, Costa, LaCosta,* and *Costard* in the existing documentation. Note as well that in the present work I use actual names (versus pseudonyms) only where the individuals have been identified in other published work.

8. Thomas (1983) and Brasseur (2009) do not report use of this tense in their own descriptions of the local varieties either. Butler (1995) also records simple past usage in the folksong repertoire of Marie Félix of L'Anse-à-Canards (1923–2011), who, like Madame LeCostard, does not use this form in storytelling or in ordinary discourse.

9. This is clearly the case for particular phonological features, such as variation in the realization of nasal vowels (as documented by King and Ryan 1991).

10. These same features are highlighted in a satiric text *La lettre de Pistache* (a surname which is probably a play on *pastiche*), published in a New Orleans newspaper in 1928 and contained in the corpus Early Louisiana French Correspondence (http://www.lib.lsu.edu/special/cffs/). See Comeau and King (2010) for discussion.

11. As we shall see later in this book, similar caution is necessary in interpreting artistic representations of Acadian French in media discourse of the early twenty-first century.

12. The same may be said of Jacques-Louis Ménétra, the eighteenth-century Parisian glazier whose memoirs ( *Journal de ma vie* [Ménétra 1998]) are of considerable interest to both social historians and French historical linguists. See Lodge (2004) for discussion.

13. This interview was deposited in the Memorial University of Newfoundland Folklore and Language Archives and given the identification Hewson C86-64. Hewson's 1964 recordings are to my knowledge the earliest French Newfoundland audio recordings made by a linguist. Note that "JS" is another Cap Saint-

George resident who took part in the interview. I thank John Hewson for providing me, many years ago, with his transcripts of these interviews.

14. This short extract includes a morphologically integrated verb of English origin, *boarder* 'to board', as well as the borrowed English intransitive preposition *back*. See King (2000) for analysis of such instances of lexical borrowing along with King (2011) for a cross-dialectal comparison of the semantic and syntactic integration of *back* in North American French varieties.

15. Interestingly, Lavandera's classic (1978) critique of Labovian variationist sociolinguistics cites Sankoff and Thibault's (1977) analysis of this very variable. Lavandera notes that for Sankoff and Thibault, copular uses of *avoir-être* do not count nor do tokens involving uncompleted actions, where *être* is the only auxiliary possible. Thus, the variable is reduced to "the one context in which they [i.e., the variants] seem not to introduce any difference in meaning and where they vary according to social and lexical constraints" (Lavandera 1978, 178). It should be noted that in subsequent decades the Labovian position (operationalized for auxiliary selection by Sankoff and Thibault) has clearly won the battle. Only contexts that admit variation are counted.

16. "On notera que le français avancé, tirant parti de la coexistence de deux auxiliares, *être* et *avoir*, au passé des verbes intransitifs, tend à leur donner des valeurs distinctes selon qu'il s'agit du parfait («état consecutif à un procès» : *être*) ou du prétérit («procès dans le passé» : *avoir*)."

17. It is clear, though, that the question of AAVE's origins has not been resolved. For work placing considerably more importance on (West African) substrate influence, see, for example, Rickford (1998, 2006) and Winford (1997, 1998).

18. I use the more neutral term *variety* in the present work. For francophone readers in particular, the term *dialect* has negative connotations, although that is certainly not the intent in the generative literature or in traditional dialectology.

19. Note, though, that Cardinaletti and Repetti (2010) present a substantially different analysis of the northern Italian dialects. They argue, contra the dominant approach, that subject clitics in these varieties actually represent a depending-marking pattern quite different from what is found elsewhere in Romance.

20. "Nous avons affaire, dans l'étude comparative des dialectes, à des systems grammaticaux extrêmement proches, qui ne different que pour un nombre restraint de propriétés fondamentales; ces propriétés sont donc relativement faciles à isoler et à démêler de toute intérférence cachée" (Rizzi 1989, 9).

21. The smaller Acadian communities are often included in census surveys with surrounding English communities. Determining the population of, say, L'Anse-à-Canards at any particular point in time requires census data to be broken down in light of data provided by community organizations and fieldwork observations. All of our 1980 consultants for the adjoining communities of Stephenville/Kippens were at that time residents of Kippens, although some had earlier lived in Stephenville proper.

22. I thank the Archives de folklore et d'ethnologie of Laval University for allowing me to copy both the sound recordings and original transcriptions of all of the Acadian data recorded by Lacourcière. The transcriptions were then corrected using the same transcription protocol as for the sociolinguistic interviews at York University.

23. Use of these data has been limited primarily to work on verb morphology, discussed in chapter 3. I thank Sylvie Dubois for access to the Louisiana corpora.

24. To give but one example, of the 26 papers included in the proceedings of a 2004 conference on North American French varieties held in France at the Université d'Avignon (Brasseur and Falkert 2005), 17 were concerned with Acadian French, and, of these, 12 were concerned wholly or in part with *chiac*, a variety spoken in the Moncton area of southeast New Brunswick.

25. I use grammatical commentary to identify broadly the time frame of decline of particular usage in France. See King, Martineau, and Mougeon (2011) for discussion of the (judicious) use of such data.

26. Indeed, the survey administrator Édmont's lead question *Comment dit-on en patois?* ('How does one say in patois?') leaves no doubt of the orientation of the survey's directors. I thank David Heap for reminding me of this fact.

## CHAPTER 3

1. Collection of Acadian folktales by both European (Geneviève Massignon) and Quebec (Luc Lacourcière) scholars would follow by the late 1940s (see Labelle 2001). The dialectal variant Cendrillouse contains the common vernacular (feminine) nominalizer written *-euse* in Standard French.

2. In his 1948 article Haden notes that LeBlanc died "prematurely" in 1943.

3. I thank the Centre d'études acadiennes of the Université de Moncton for making a copy of this recording available to me.

4. Relative *qui* does not display palatalization of the initial consonant, outside of fixed expressions such as *l'année qui vient* 'next year' (Flikeid 1989b). This pattern is also noted by Haden (1948).

5. We would expect to find the *être* auxiliary with passives, which are absent from the text.

6. In the Acadian interlinear glosses, I translate *je* as 1PERS rather than 'I' for varieties which retain the traditional morphology of the verb since use of *je* in combination with a *-ons* inflectional ending renders the verb first-person plural.

7. *En frais de* is a longstanding Acadian variant of *en train de* (Cormier 1999).

8. The auxiliary verb *avoir* may be rendered *ont* in the third-person plural in both standard and vernacular French, while the unambiguously vernacular form is *avont* (Flikeid 1994). Two *-ont* tokens were not included in this count as they are ambiguous. Further, the synthetic future takes *-ont* in the third-person

plural in both standard and vernacular French. Such tokens were likewise not included in this count.

9.   Gender agreement with *tous* 'all' is uncommon in both Acadian and Lauren-tian vernaculars. *Tout* [tʊt] is usually invariable as in *tous* [tʊt] *les garçons* 'all the boys', *je l'ai tout* [tʊt] *fait* 'I did everything' (see Lemieux, Saint-Amour, and Sankoff 1985; Péronnet 1991). The *tous* [tu] pronunciation here (as indicated by the accompanying phonetic transcription) is unexpected. In regular French orthography, the verb *assayer* is written *essayer*.

10.  Haden (1948, 32) wrongly classifies this token as an instance of the simple past, which, as noted in chapter 2, is homophonous with the imperfect subjunctive in these varieties. Ryan (1981) argues that from a Martinet (functionalist) per-spective that there is no reason to distinguish the simple past and the imperfect subjunctive in Acadian French, classifying what I am calling imperfect subjunc-tive tokens as instances of the simple past. He overtly disagrees with Gesner's characterization of similar Baie Sainte-Marie, Nova Scotia, data. However, when a sufficiently large data set is considered and the relevant constraints on usage established quantitatively, it becomes apparent that the simple past and the imperfect subjunctive are in fact distinct. For example, it is clear in the Butler Grosse Coques corpus that the matrix verb *vouloir* triggers both the present and the imperfect subjunctive. See Comeau (2011) for detailed analysis of subjunc-tive usage in this variety.

11.  *Chus* is a dialectal variant of standard *chez*, to be discussed in chapter 4. We find here *couri*, the (regularized) vernacular past participle of *courir*, not Standard French *couru*.

12.  Haden (1948) cites *se ranger* as the dialectal equivalent of *rentrer* 'to go home'.

13.  As noted in chapter 2, the phrase *il dit* is ambiguous in that it may be an instance of simple past or historic present; all 10 such tokens were excluded.

14.  Unlike narratives of personal experience, traditional folktales are not a very good source for this particular variable, since first-person plural reference will only occur in reported speech.

15.  In reading Massignon's (1947) article more than six decades later, one cannot help but be struck by the singularity of her accomplishment as a woman travel-ing around rural Atlantic Canada in the late 1940s. As for Massignon's lack of commentary on the use of the inflected future, this is understandable since its alleged decline was subject to little commentary before the second half of the twentieth century; the lack of mention of distinctive third-person plural verbal morphology is, however, curious.

16.  Both texts show *ne* absence at a very high rate, for an average of 80.5% ($n = 159$). For this particular feature, Martineau and Mougeon (2003) suggest that *ne* absence is a relatively recent (nineteenth century) development in both Laurentian and Metropolitan French.

17.  Comeau and King (2011) analyze a made-for-adults animated television series about an Acadian superhero Acadieman, which is set in southeastern New Brunswick. In the series, *ils...ont* is used extensively but *je...ons* is entirely

absent. The same is true for a series of comic books (LeBlanc 2007, 2009) based on the same character.

18. See Brunot (1966) for a discussion of homophony between the simple past and the imperfect subjunctive in the history of the language.

19. I thank Yves Charles Morin for bringing this source to my attention.

20. For grammatical questions in the atlas survey, informants were asked to translate into their local variety (*Comment dit-on en patois?*, noted above). While this may seem a rather dubious elicitation device for modern researchers, its success is evidenced in the wide variety of responses given on the corresponding atlas maps.

21. I refer the reader to Comeau's (2011) detailed treatment of the forms of the subjunctive in Baie Sainte-Marie Acadian French. Comeau found present, past, and imperfect subjunctive to display remarkably little variation and to be quite productive. When the right semantic conditions are in place, the appropriate form of the subjunctive is selected at very high rates.

22. I define morphological richness in terms of what exists in varieties of French, diachronically and synchronically. To the Romanist familiar with languages such as Provençal, varieties of French may, on the contrary, seem rather impoverished.

23. These very high percentages mask one important point of variation in the system, number agreement in a particular construction, subject relative clauses, which will be examined in some detail in chapter 4.

24. King, Nadasdi, and Butler (2004) argue that in the Abram-Village variety *je...ons* use is more subtle than this; it is actually reevaluated as a performance key (in the sense of Bauman 1977), used to index the performance of narratives of personal or community experience.

25. Note that vernacular French often has just one third-person plural pronoun. In my own and in Gary Butler's Acadian French corpora, standard third-person plural feminine *elles* is unattested.

26. Beaulieu and Balcom (1998) also argue that subject clitics have become agreement markers in this variety (as has been argued by Auger 1994 and Roberge 1990 for Quebec French). I will not present their arguments here, but point the reader to my own work in this regard on the Newfoundland variety, wherein I argue that the subject clitics remain clitics, as in Standard French (King and Nadasdi 1997).

27. The orthographic choice here indicates that Cajun (like Atlantic Canada Acadian) French preserves pronunciation of the final consonant, lost in Standard French pronunciation but retained by standard orthographic <x>.

28. *Connaître* and *savoir* are basically distinguished by the former involving knowledge of a person or place, the latter knowledge of a fact. However, Dubois's (1997) sociolinguistic corpus abounds with use of the Cajun discourse marker *tu connais* 'you know' where all other French varieties of which I am aware have *tu sais*. This suggests that distinction has been lost in Louisiana varieties.

Indeed, the *Dictionary of Louisiana French* (2010) gives both meanings for both verbs.

29. This is a phenomenon whereby both /ʃ/ and /ʒ/ are realized with velar or glottal variants, linked to, but not limited to, the old *centre-ouest* province of Saintonge. Chidaine (1967) reports that the *saintongeais* variants are in widespread use "en Acadie" in the Acadian-settled Beauce County and Lac St-Jean in Quebec, while Falkert (2005, 79) notes its presence in the French of les Îles-de-la-Madeleine. Lucci (1972, 95) likewise discusses these variants in southeastern New Brunswick. Flikeid (1994), however, reports that this feature has been retained only in Baie Sainte-Marie and part of Île-Madame in Nova Scotia. It remains quite common in Newfoundland varieties (King 1989).

30. Rottet (2001, 151–52) presents evidence from early Louisiana sources that this loss was at least in part due to variation (and possible confusion) over whether the referent was singular or plural.

31. Third-person feminine singular has *elle* for both the clitic and the strong pronoun; the same homophony is true of second-person plural *vous*.

32. There is some debate regarding the utility or veracity of grammatical commentary as a source of sociolinguistic evidence, with researchers such as Poplack and Dion (2009) suggesting that such data are at best unreliable. I personally take a different position: that grammatical commentary, USED JUDICIOUSLY, can illuminate patterns of variation and change. By way of example, see King, Martineau, and Mougeon's (2011) study of the evolution of first-person plural pronominal usage in European French, which shows a convergence of data from grammatical commentary, theatrical representations of the spoken language, and dialectological and sociolinguistic data.

33. Use of the pronominal verb *s'en aller* is actually a more conservative variant of the periphrastic future than bare *aller* + infinitive. In the initial stages of analysis of the Acadian data, King and Nadasdi (2003) kept the two variants separate. Note that in the interlinear glosses for a particular variety, I only include person for the verb if that variety actually makes a distinction: the Newfoundland variety which provide the data here have [va] throughout the singular present indicative for *aller*, so person is not indicated on the verb's gloss.

34. I consider *il y a* 'there are' to be a lexicalized expression in Acadian French since it is the only construction in which the preverbal clitic *y* occurs. For instance, *je pense à lui* 'I think about him' does not have an equivalent in *j'y pense* nor does *je vais* (or *va*) *là* 'I go there' in *j'y vais*.

35. Of course, following standard practice, fixed expressions have also been omitted, since they do not admit variation. Note that Chevalier's (1996) study of the use of future tense morphology in the language use of southeastern New Brunswick university students is not directly comparable to our own study, since she (deliberately) includes both habituals and true futures.

36. The futurate present did not enter into the quantitative analysis here because it occurred relatively infrequently in the data set.

37. Roberts (2011) also finds a significant result for polarity in his variationist study of Metropolitan French. However, since his study is based on the Beeching corpus of spoken Metropolitan French, which combines data from a wide variety of sources (it includes data for a variety of spoken genres and data from the Paris region and Brittany in northen France as well as from Lot and Minervois in the south), it is difficult to interpret these results. At the time of writing, this corpus was available for download at http://www.llas.ac.uk/resources/mb/80. Note that in all sociolinguistic corpora studied to date, the number of affirmative tokens far outweigh the negative polarity tokens: with a mixed-source corpus, it is particularly difficult to evaluate findings based heavily on a small number of (negative polarity) tokens.

38. Excluded from this study were less frequently occurring ways of expressing past temporal reference, such as the pluperfect (*plus-que-parfait*) and the compound past tense (*passé surcomposé*).

39. We were able to distinguish the homophonous simple past and imperfect subjunctive as follows: we first determined the subjunctive-selecting verbal and adverbial matrices for this variety with respect to the present subjunctive. Since particular subjunctive contexts might have been missing from the Grosses Coques corpus, we added such contexts found in our other Acadian corpora. We then used native-speaker judgments to determine whether or not they should be added to the list for Grosses Coques. When the exercise was complete, I removed all data involving homophonous tokens (i.e., they could be instances of the simple past or the imperfect subjunctive) that occurred in what we had identified as subjunctive-selecting contexts, leaving only unambiguous simple past tense usage.

40. Cichocki's (2011) analysis of degree of retention of traditional phonetic features of Acadian French, based on statistical analysis of data from the 1998 *Atlas linguistique du vocabulaire maritime acadien* (Péronnet et al. 1998), found such features to be more strongly present in the southeast than in the northeast of New Brunswick.

## CHAPTER 4

1. Contexts that admit variation include complement clauses, relative clauses, and the broad category labeled circumstantial clauses by traditional grammars.

2. The Héroard diary is one of the key representations of seventeenth-century French. Over a period of several years, Héroard recorded, ostensibly verbatim, the Dauphin's (future king's) speech and that of some of his servants.

3. Huot (1992; cited by Blanche-Benveniste 1995, 129) notes that *il est probable que* is also attested with the subjunctive in late-twentieth-century French.

4. See Longobardi (2001) for an important formal (Minimalist) account of the European history of French *chez*.

5. While *à la maison de* is attested early on in the history of French (Littré 1968; cited by Mougeon and Beniak 1991, 169), these latter authors make a strong case that it died out in the language and that the Ontario French usage of this variant that they document is actually an innovation. Although they do not draw our attention to this fact, Mougeon and Beniak's quantitative data show that when *su* is used, it is always with a lexical complement.

6. Note that *su* 'at the house of' is homophonous with the preposition *su* 'on'.

7. The *est-ce que* construction was regarded as a feature of spoken language more so than written by European commentators well into the twentieth century (Blanche-Benveniste 1995, 138). However, Elsig (2009) suggests that the *est-ce que* variant is being supplanted by use of the *tu* (< *ti*) question particle in the French of Quebec's Gatineau region (as attested in the Poplack Ottawa-Hull sociolinguistic corpus). Of course, yes/no questions may also be signaled by rising intonation, as in informal registers of all varieties of spoken French of which I am aware.

8. See Rowlett (2007, 198–209) for a discussion of formal treatments of these cases of movement and their similarities to and differences from English subject-auxiliary inversion.

9. Roberts (1993) notes that similar developments took place in varieties of Franco-Provençal and in Catalan (Roberts cites Wheeler 1988 with regard to Catalan).

10. It is the only variant found in the corpora examined by Elsig (2009) (for contemporary French, he used the 1982 Ottawa-Hull corpus). However, it would be rather surprising to me if a variant documented in the variety up to the mid-twenieth century (i.e., *ti*) had disappeared completely from isolated rural areas.

11. See Vinet (2001) for an overview and formal account of the uses of the *tu* particle in Quebec French.

12. Use of the *vous* pronoun in interrogatives is fairly infrequent in the Grosses Coques corpus, but when it does occur there is pronominal inversion. This example comes from a narrative of personal experience: *dit* may be either present tense or simple past (see chapter 2 in this regard).

13. See Comeau (2008) for a minimalist account of Acadian intercommunity variation for yes/no question formation.

14. This example comes from reported speech in L'Anse-à-Canards renowned conteur Émile Benoît's performance of *La montagne noire* 'The Black Mountain' (AT 313 "The Girl as Helper in the Hero's Flight"). I have also heard second-person pronominal inversion in L'Anse-à-Canards, but only used to address community outsiders.

15. Note that the *ti* question marker may also be used in exclamations, as in *J'avais ti peur!* 'Wasn't I afraid!' This is also true of the *tu* variant (see Vinet 2001 for Quebec French).

16. I thank Louise Beaulieu for providing me with these examples from her FANENB corpus.

17. This is, in fact, what I have done for the Prince Edward Island corpora. The community-interviewers' speech was analyzed for a number of variables to ensure that their own usage was in line with that of the interviewers. Once this was determined to be the case, I extracted data from interviewer questions for analysis. Obviously, this is only possible where the interviewer is a true insider. The Grosses Coques and L'Anse-à-Canards corpora contained many group interviews, and both consultants and interviewers provided a range of interrogative data.

18. The third-person singular and plural pronominal forms *il* and *ils* tend to be homophonous in colloquial French. This is the case for Newfoundland Acadian, where *ils* is never realized with [z] in liaison contexts (e.g., *ils arrivont* [ilarivõ] 'they arrive') in my corpora. Similarly, *ils* with a [z] of liaison is at least unusual in Prince Edward Island French, as it is in the New Brunswick and Nova Scotia varieties, as evidenced by Flikeid and Péronnet's (1989) orthographic choice *il* for the third-person plural pronoun.

19. Such usage overlaps with Standard French. However, given that such forms occur in a number of varieties where exposure to the standard through schooling ranges from heavy to nonexistent, I refrain from labeling them as standard since they also occur in many colloquial French varieties.

20. As in many other colloquial French varieties, relative *qui* reduces to *qu'* [k] in the environment before a vowel, thus patterning with the *que* complementizer (e.g., *Je sais qu'il a parti* 'I know that he has left'). We shall see below that relative *qui* is best regarded as a variant of the *que* complementizer.

21. Cornips and Corrigan (2005) discuss in detail the problem of low frequency of occurrence in corpora for particular types of (morpho)syntactic variables, along with some ways around it.

22. While it is not clear whether *it*-clefts are frozen expressions or are indeed generated by the grammar, their influence on these results is obviously minimal.

23. As there were only 12 instances of *il y en a* initially considered here, additional data for these speakers and for several other residents of L'Anse-à-Canards were added to the present analysis of *il y en a* structures. Like the other eight speakers, none had been educated in French, none had achieved more than secondary education, and none worked outside the community.

24. In Newfoundland Acadian, the third-person singular of the verb *partir* 'to leave' is the regularized form *partit*, not Standard French *part*. Some accounts of the Newfoundland variety treat *partit* as if it were an instance of the simple past, which is in fact absent from the variety, as noted in chapter 3.

25. Newfoundland Acadian provides additional evidence of a distinction between the two in that interrogative *qui* and relative *qui* differ in their phonetic realization. Interrogative *qui* undergoes the typically Acadian phonological process whereby velar stops palatalize to become affricates before non–low front vowels; relative *qui* does not undergo this process. To my knowledge, this distinction exists in all Acadian varieties that still have palatalization of velar stops (Lucci 1972).

26. Under early Minimalism (Chomsky 1992), verbs would come fully inflected in the lexicon.

27. For clarity of exposition, I simplify the tree, leaving out, for example, vP.

28. Under the Pesetsky and Torrego (2001) analysis, it is unclear why T moves to C but the verb (which in French raises to T, under V-to-T Movement) does not.

29. Adger (2006, 523–24) develops a somewhat different (Minimalist) account of my data within his Combinatorial Variability model, one which also turns on feature underspecification and late insertion.

30. King and Nadasdi (1996) presents complete results for Prince Edward Island. This study considers, along with community, a number of other social factors, including level of French language education and position in the linguistic marketplace.

31. Perrot (1995) discusses default agreement in the speech of southeastern New Brunswick adolescents. However, her results are not readily comparable to the other studies mentioned here because no quantitative analysis of variation was undertaken.


## CHAPTER 5

1. Following from Burzio (1986), unaccusative verbs' single argument merges as a direct object, to which they do not assign a thematic role. On the other hand, unergative verbs' single argument merges as a subject, to which they assign an agent thematic role. The contrast is exemplified by Standard French *il est mort* (*mourir* 'to die') versus *il a téléphoné* (*téléphoner* 'to telephone'). Note that cross-linguistically, the passive auxiliary is typically *be* (and never *have*).

2. While Italian, Occitan, Sardinian, and Rheto-Romance maintain auxiliary alternation for intransitive verbs, it has been lost in Picard, Wallon, Catalan, Portuguese, Spanish, and Romanian, where the *have* auxiliary has won out (Rideout 2011, 3).

3. Fournier (1998, 256–60) lists the following verbs as exhibiting variable auxiliary selection in Classical French: *apparaître* 'to appear', *cesser* 'to cease', *choir* 'to drop', *courir* 'to run', *croître* 'to increase in number, volume', *déchoir* 'to deprive', *demeurer* 'to live (somewhere)', *descendre* 'to go down', *disparaître* 'to disappear', *entrer* 'to enter', *monter* 'to go up', *partir* 'to leave', *rentrer* 'to return (home)', *rester* 'to stay', *retourner* 'to return', *sortir* 'to go out', and *tomber* 'to fall down'.

4. These dialect grammars and glossaries are not particularly helpful for usage with intransitive verbs since when they say there is variable usage, we cannot be sure if they include what most present-day linguists would consider copular constructions. See chapter 2 for discussion.

5. *The Dictionary of Louisiana French* (2010, 52) gives a similar example under the entry for *avoir*: *Il s'avait mis une petite calotte comme dans le vieux temps* 'He had put on a little beanie cap like in the old days'. The dictionary also attests to variable

auxiliary selection with intransitives, a tendency confirmed by my own examination of Dubois's (1994) sociolinguistic interviews for older speakers from
Lafourche Parish. Why Louisiana Cajun variety would present greater usage of
*être* than do Atlantic Canada Acadian varieties is not clear.

6. Unfortunately, Beniak and Mougeon (1989) report only percentages with no
raw numbers, which causes some difficulty in interpreting the magnitude of
their findings. Gillian Sankoff (pers. comm., Oct. 28, 2012) reports that use of
*avoir* with pronominal verbs is absent from the Montreal French corpus. King's
(2013) study of auxiliary selection in the Grosses Coques, Nova Scotia, corpus
confirms the results of Gesner's smaller study: *avoir* use is categorical with the
set of verbs in table 5.1.

7. *Se dégreyer* is derived from the verb *gréer*, a nautical term meaning 'to equip a
ship' that has generalized in Acadian (and probably other maritime) varieties,
including Louisiana French, to include the meaning 'to get dressed'.

8. It is worth noting that descriptions of twentieth-century Picard (e.g., Auger
2003) give only the *have* auxiliary.

9. Rayside is now incorporated into the town of Sudbury.

10. It should be noted that the aim of the Moncton initiatives is not to denigrate
the local variety but to help students attain competence in the written norm.
See Balcom (2008) for discussion and references. Note as well that while use of
*être* increased with instruction, even first-year students used this auxiliary with
pronominal verbs, going against community norms.

11. I have argued elsewhere (King 1991) that while *ce-que* may have originated as a
reduced form of *est-ce-que* 'is it that' in colloquial French, in Acadian French it
is the allomorph of complementizer *que* that appears in cases of *wh*-movement
(recall that Acadian French has so-called doubly filled COMP). Note as well
that while French has *sur* 'on' (Acadian *su(r)*, see chapter 4) when there is an
overt complement of the preposition, *dessus* is found elsewhere. *Sous* 'below'
and *dessous*, along with *dans* 'in' and *dedans*, present the same contrast.

12. In this variety, the first-person singular future ending is pronounced [e], while
the first-person singular conditional ending (of *je ferais*) would be pronounced
[a]. In other words, the two are not homophonous, as in many other varieties
of French, and we know that it is indeed the future (*je ferai*) used here.

13. Similarly, in contact Spanish only calques involving the extension of *para atrás*
on an English model are found (Silva-Corvalán 1994; Lipski 1990; both cited
by Rottet 2000).

14. The fact that speakers were responding to a translation task explains the relationship between (26) and (28) and between (27) and (29).

15. Rottet's examples show singular/plural alternation in the form of singular *ton*
(m.)/*ta* (f.) versus plural *tes* for the second-person plural possessive pronoun.
However, as examples (26) and (28) show, in the second-person plural *votre*
(sg.) corresponds to the homophonous *votres* (pl.) where all other French varieties of which I am aware would have *votre* versus *vos*.

16. Rottet uses *il* rather than *ils* to orthographically represent the third-person plural subject pronoun presumably because the [z] of liaison found in Standard French is not realized in this variety. It is likewise infrequent in varieties of Atlantic Canada Acadian French, and many Acadian linguists use the same spelling, as noted earlier. Similarly, *jha* in (30) is a representation of the /ʃ/ *saintongeais* pronunciation for the lexical item *ça*.

17. See Bouchard (1982), Vinet (1984), and King and Roberge (1990) for technical details of these analyses.

## CHAPTER 6

1. There is a substantial body of sociolinguistic research on intensifiers in contemporary English: see, for example, Macauley (2006) for contemporary Glasgow English, Bucholtz et al. (2007) for California English, Tagliamonte and Roberts (2005) for U.S. (media) English.

2. At the time of writing, the following url allowed access to this collection's electronic database: http://www.tlfq.ulaval.ca/.

3. It may be that *wayment* is also derived from *moyennement* [mwenmã] > [wemã]. Individual speakers use both *wellment* and *wayment* and write them as I have written them here.

4. Meechan and Poplack (1995) made an important methodological breakthrough by quantitatively comparing the behavior of single-word tokens to that of unproblematic tokens from the same corpus (i.e., to unambiguous multiword code-switches, unmixed English language material, and unambiguous French language material) according to several diagnostics. The method has been successfully tested for several pairs of genetically unrelated languages involved in mixing, such as Wolof/French and Fongbe/French (Meechan and Poplack 1995). This method can profitably be applied to languages that are genetically quite similar, as shown by Turpin's (1998) application to southeast New Brunswick Acadian data involving French-English language mixture.

5. I reproduce Chevalier and Hudson's (2005) transcription conventions for their Acadian data.

6. Comeau (2007) gives a full account of yet another borrowed intensifier, *tight*, in this variety, as in *Il est apeuré tight* 'He is really scared'. Comeau argues that such usage involves an extension of meaning from that of the English resultative predicate as found in 'to shut tight', 'to lock tight', etc.

7. I leave the formal explicit analysis of the English modifier *quite* as an open question.

8. *Putain* literally means 'whore' while *crisse* < *Christ*. See Vincent (1984) for discussion of religion-based swearing (*les sacres*) in Laurentian French.

9. Grevisse describes this form of gender agreement as an example of the colloquial language that was creeping into more formal French.

10. In fact, in English, I would place emphasis on *funny* (*a FUNNY story*) to get this meaning.

11. Obviously, *beaucoup* is neither a noun nor an adjective, but it does resemble *quite* in meaning.

12. I thank Raymond Mougeon for discussion the limits of this construction in European French with me.

13. See King (1991, 2000) for a formal analysis of the linear sequences found in the Prince Edward Island varieties. Note that even among my most advanced consultants, lone English *wh*-words *who, what, where,* and the like are not used, which, from my reading of the literature, is also the case in southeastern New Brunswick. The one exception is *why,* also found (albeit rarely) in the Prince Edward Island corpus. The use of English-origin *why* may be understood from the point of view of current grammatical theory: Rizzi (1990) argues that *why* is a clausal adjunct. Cross-linguistically, *why* seems to be an unreliable diagnostic for the landing site of general "well-behaved" *wh*-phrases. In a number of languages, including Spanish (Suñer 1994; Zubizarreta 1998), Romanian (Gabriela Alboiu, pers. comm., Oct. 17, 2007), and Hungarian (Kiss 1998), there is a requirement that, while *wh*-phrases have to be adjacent to the highest verbal head, *why* can instead be followed by topics.

14. A person/number effect has likewise been found in prior studies of other varieties (e.g., Sankoff 1980, for Montreal French and Martineau 1988 and Dion 2003 for Ottawa-Hull French).

## CHAPTER 7

1. "[E]ntre 1980 et 1985, en l'espace de cinq ans seulement, plus de soixante-quinze etudes de linguistique acadienne ont vu le jour et plusieurs projets de recherché, dont certains de grande envergure, [était] en cours" (Gesner 1986, 1).

# REFERENCES

Aarne, Antti. 1961. *The Types of the Folktale: A Classification and Bibliography*. Translated and enlarged by Stith Thompson. 2nd revision. FF (Folklore Fellows) Communications, no. 184. Helsinki: Academia Scientirum Fennica.

Adger, David. 2006. "Combinatorial Variability." *Journal of Linguistics* 42.3: 503–30. doi:10.1017/S002222670600418X.

Adger, David, and Jennifer Smith. 2005. "Variation and the Minimalist Program." In Cornips and Corrigan, 149–78.

Agha, Asif. 2003. "The Social Life of Cultural Value." In "Word and Beyond: Linguistic and Semiotic Studies of Sociocultural Order," edited by Paul Manning. Special issue, *Language and Communication* 23.3–4: 231–73. doi:10.1016/S0271-5309(03)00012-0.

Allard, Réal, and Rodrigue Landry. 1998. "French in New Brunswick." In *Language in Canada*, edited by John Edwards, 202–25. Cambridge: Cambridge University Press. doi:10.1017/CBO9780511620829.012.

Andry de Boisregard, Nicolas. 1689. *Réflexions sur l'usage présent de la langue françoise; ou, remarques nouvelles et critiques touchant la politesse du langage*. Paris: d'Houry.

Arrivé, Michel, Françoise Gadet, and Michel Galmiche. 1986. *La grammaire d'aujourd'hui: Guide alphabétique de linguistique française*. Paris: Flammarion.

Arsenault, Georges. 1987. *Les Acadiens de l'Île, 1720–1980*. Moncton, N.B.: Éditions d'Acadie.

Auger, Julie. 1994. "Pronominal Clitics in Colloquial French: A Morphological Analysis." Ph.D. diss., University of Pennsylvania.

———. 2003. "Le redoublement des sujets en picard." *Journal of French Language Studies* 13.3: 381–404. doi:10.1017/S0959269503001200.

———. 2005. "Un bastion francophone en Amérique du Nord: Le Québec." In Valdman, Auger, and Piston-Hatlen 2005, 39–80.

Balcom, Patricia. 2008. "On the Learning of Auxiliary Use in the Referential Variety by Speakers of New Brunswick Acadian French." *Canadian Journal of Linguistics* 53.1: 7–34. doi:10.1353/cjl.0.0003.

Bauche, Henri. 1920. *Le langage populaire: Grammaire, syntaxe et dictionnaire du français tel qu'on le parle dans le peuple de Paris, avec tous les termes d'argot usuel*. Paris: Payot. 4th ed., 1946.

Bauman, Richard. 1977. *Verbal Art as Performance*. Prospect Heights, Ill.: Waveland Press.

Beaulieu, Louise. 1994. "Une analyse sociolinguistique du pronom *Wh* inanimé dans les relatives libres dans le français acadien du nord-est du Nouveau-Brunswick." *Linguistica Atlantica* 15: 39–68.

———. 1996. "'Qui se ressemble s'assemble' et à s'assembler on finit par se ressembler: Une analyse sociolinguistique de la variable *si/si que* en français acadien du nord-est du Nouveau-Brunswick." In Dubois and Boudreau 1996, 91–111.

Beaulieu, Louise, and Patricia Balcom. 1998. "Le statut des pronoms personnels sujets en français acadien du nord-est du Nouveau-Brunswick." *Linguistica Atlantica* 20: 1–27.

Beaulieu, Louise, and Wladyslaw Cichocki. 2003. "Grammaticalisation et perte des marques d'accord sujet-verbe en français acadien du Nord-Est." In *Papers from the 26th Annual Meeting of the Atlantic Provinces Linguistic Association*, edited by Sandra Clarke, 121–43. St. John's: Memorial University of Newfoundland.

———. 2008. "La flexion postverbale *-ont* en français acadien: Une analyse sociolinguistique." *La revue canadienne de linguistique* 53.1: 35–62. doi:10.1353/cjl.0.0005.

Beniak, Édouard, and Raymond Mougeon. 1989. "Recherches sociolinguistiques sur la variabilité en français ontarien." In Mougeon and Beniak 1989, 69–103.

Benveniste, Émile 1959. "Les relations de temps dans le verbe français." *Bulletin de la Société de Linguistique de Paris* 54: 69–82. Reprinted in *Problèmes de linguistique générale*, vol. 1, 237–50. Paris: Gallimard, 1966.

Bernard, Lorene Marie. 1933. "A Study of Louisiana French in Lafayette Parish." Master's thesis, Louisiana State University.

Blanche-Benveniste, Claire. 1995. "Quelques faits de syntaxe." In *Histoire de la langue française, 1914–45*, edited by Gérald Antoine and Robert Martin, 125–52. Paris: Éditions du CNRS.

Borsley, Robert D., Maggie Tallerman, and David Willis. 2007. *The Syntax of Welsh.* Cambridge: Cambridge University Press.

Bouchard, Denis. 1982. "Les constructions relatives en français vernaculaire et en français standard: Étude d'un paramètre." In *La syntaxe comparée du français standard et populaire: Approches formelle et fonctionnelle*, edited by Claire Lefebvre, 103–34. Quebec: Office de la langue française.

Bourdieu, Pierre, and Luc Boltanski. 1975. "Le fétishisme de la langue." *Actes de la recherche en sciences sociales* 1.4: 2–32. doi:10.3406/arss.1975.3417.

Brandi, Luciana, and Patrizia Cordin. 1989. "Two Italian Dialects and the Null Subject Parameter." In *The Null Subject Parameter*, edited by Osvaldo Jaeggli and Kenneth J. Safir, 111–42. Dordrecht: Kluwer.

Brasseaux, Carl A. 1998. "Acadian Settlement Patterns, 1765–1900." In *Creoles and Cajuns: French Louisiana*, edited by Wolfgang Binder, 17–32. New York: Peter Lang.

Brasseur, Patrice. 2001. *Dictionnaire des régionalismes du français de Terre-Neuve*. Tübingen: Niemeyer.

———. 2009. "La régularisation des paradigmes verbaux en franco-terre-neuvien." *Langue et société* 127: 85–102. doi:10.3917/ls.127.0085.

Brasseur, Patrice, and Anika Falkert, eds. 2005. *Français d'Amérique: Approches morphosyntaxiques; Actes du colloque international Grammaire comparée des variétés de français d'Amérique, Université d'Avignon, 17–20 mai 2004.* Paris: L'Harmattan.

Brown, Becky. 1986. "Cajun/English Code-Switching: A Test of Formal Models." In *Diversity and Diachrony*, edited by David Sankoff, 399–406. Amsterdam: Benjamins.

———. 1993. "The Social Consequences of Writing Lousiana French." *Language in Society* 22.1: 67–102. doi:10.1017/S0047404500016924.

Brunot, Ferdinand. 1966. *Histoire de la langue française des origines à nos jours.* Edited by Gérald Antoine. Paris: Colin.

Bucholtz, Mary, Nancy Bermudez, Victor Fung, Lisa Edwards, and Rosalva Vargas. 2007. "Hella Nor Cal or Totally So Cal? The Perceptual Dialectology of California." *Journal of English Linguistics* 35.4: 325–352. doi:10.1177/0075424207 307780.

Burnett, Heather Susan. 2008. "Sur la définition de 'adverbe' et la nécéssité du marquage syntaxique catégoriel." Paper presented at the annual meeting of the Canadian Linguistics Association, Vancouver, B.C., May 31–June 2.

Burzio, Luigi. 1986. *Italian Syntax: A Government-Binding Approach.* Dordrecht: Kluwer.

Butler, Gary R. 1990. *Saying Isn't Believing: Conversational Narrative and the Discourse of Tradition in a French-Newfoundland Community.* St. John's: Institute for Social and Economic Research, Memorial University of Newfoundland.

———. 1995. *Histoire et traditions orales des Franco-Acadiens de Terre-Neuve.* Sillery, Que.: Septentrion.

Canale, Michael, Raymond Mougeon, Monique Bélanger, and Christine Main. 1977. "Recherches en dialectologie franco-ontarienne." *Travaux de recherches sur le bilinguisme* 14: 1–20.

Cardinaletti, Anna, and Lori Repetti. 2010. "Proclitic vs Enclitic Pronouns in Northern Italian Dialects and the Null-Subject Parameter." In D'Alessandro, Ledgeway, and Roberts, 119–34.

Charbonneau, Hubert, and André Guillemette. 1994. "Les pionniers du Canada au 17e siècle." In Mougeon and Beniak 1994, 59–78.

Chauveau, Jean-Paul. 2009. "Le verbe acadien, concordances européennes." In *Français du Canada–Français de France VIII: Actes du huitième colloque international, Trèves, du 12 au 15 avril 2007,* edited by Beatrice Bagola and Hans-J. Niederehe, 35–56. Tübingen: Max Niemeyer Verlag.

Chevalier, Gisèle. 1996. "L'emploi des formes du futur dans le parler acadien du sud-est du Nouveau-Brunswick." In Dubois and Boudreau 1996, 75–89.

———. 2002. "La concurrence entre «ben» et «well» en chiac du sud-est du Nouveau-Brunswick (Canada)." In "Langues en contact: Canada-Bretagne," edited by Christian Leray and Francis Manzano. *Cahiers de linguistiques* (Rennes University Press) 7: 65–81.

Chevalier, Gisèle, and Chantal Hudson. 2005. "Deux cousins en français québécois et en chiac de Moncton: *Right* et *full.*" In Brasseur and Falkert, 289–302.

Chevalier, Gisèle, and Michael Long. 2005. "*Finder out, pour qu'on les frig pas up, comment c'qu'i workont out*: Les verbes à particules en chiac." In Brasseur and Falkert, 201–12.

Chidaine, Jean G. 1967. "CH et J en saintongeais et en français canadien." In *Études de linguistique franco-canadienne: Communications présentées au XXXIVe Congrès de l'Association canadienne-française pour l'avancement des sciences, Québec, novem-*

*bre 1966*, edited by Jean-Denis Gendron and Georges Straka, 125–41. Paris: Klincksieck.

Chomsky, Noam. 1992. *A Minimalist Program for Linguistic Theory*. Cambridge, Mass.: MIT Working Papers in Linguistics.

———. 2001. "Derivation by Phase." In *Ken Hale: A Life in Language*, edited by Michael Kenstowicz, 1–52. Cambridge, Mass.: MIT Press.

Choquette, Leslie. 1997. *De français à paysans: Modernité et tradition dans le peuplement du Canada français*. Paris: Presses de l'Université Paris-Sorbonne.

Cichocki, Wladyslaw. 2011. "Retention of Traditional Phonetic Features in Acadian French." Paper presented in the DLLL Lecture Series in Linguistics and Applied Linguistics, York University, Toronto, Mar. 24.

Comeau, Philip. 2007. "The Integration of Words of English Origin in Baie Sainte-Marie Acadian French." M.A. Major Research Paper, York University.

———. 2008. "L'emploi de *-ti* comme marqueur d'interrogation en français acadien." Paper presented at Les français d'ici, University of Ottawa, May 22–25.

———. 2011. "A Window on the Past, a Move toward the Future: Sociolinguistic and Formal Perspectives on Variation in Acadian French." Ph.D. diss., York University.

Comeau, Philip, and Ruth King. 2006. "Subject Pronouns in Grosses Coques, Nova Scotia Acadian French." Unpublished ms.

———. 2010. "Variation morphosyntaxique dans deux corpus franco-louisianais." In *Une histoire épistolaire de la Louisiane*, edited by Sylvie Dubois with Albert Camp, Aaron Emmitte, Jane Richardson, and Kathryn Watson, 61–74. Quebec: Presses de l'Université Laval.

———. 2011. "Media Representations of Minority French: Valorization, Identity, and the *Acadieman* Phenomenon." *Canadian Journal of Linguistics* 56.2: 179–202. doi:10.1353/cjl.2011.0018.

Comeau, Philip, Ruth King, and Gary R. Butler. 2012. "New Insights on an Old Rivalry: The *Passé Simple* and the *Passé Composé* in Spoken Acadian French." *Journal of French Language Studies* 22.3: 315–43. doi:10.1017/S0959269511000524.

Conwell, Marilyn J., and Alphonse Juilland. 1963. *Louisiana French Grammar I: Phonology, Morphology, and Syntax*. The Hague: Mouton.

Cormier, Yves. 1999. *Dictionnaire du français acadien*. Saint-Laurent, Quebec: Fides.

Cornips, Leonie, and Karen Corrigan. 2005. "Toward an Integrated Approach to Syntactic Variation: A Retrospective and Prospective Synopsis." In *Syntax and Variation: Reconciling the Biological and the Social*, edited by Leonie Cornips and Karen P. Corrigan, 1–27. Amsterdam: Benjamins.

Côté, Marie-Hélène. 2001. "On the Status of Subject Clitics in Child French." In *Research on Child Language Acquisition: Proceedings of the 8th Conference of the International Association for the Study of Child Language*, edited by Margareta Almgren, Andoni Barreña, María-José Ezeizabarrena, Itziar Idiazabal, and Brian MacWhinney, 1314–30. Somerville, Mass.: Cascadilla.

Coupland, Nikolas. 2007. *Style: Language Variation and Identity*. Cambridge: Cambridge University Press.

Culbertson, Jennifer. 2010. "Convergent Evidence for Categorical Change in French: From Subject Clitic to Agreement Marker." *Language* 86.1: 85–132. doi:10.1353/lan.0.0183.

Daigle, Jean, ed. 1980. *Les Acadiens des Maritimes: Études thématiques*. Moncton, N.B.: Centre d'Études acadiennes.

D'Alessandro, Roberta, Adam Ledgeway, and Ian Roberts, eds. 2010. *Syntactic Variation: The Dialects of Italy*. Cambridge: Cambridge University Press.

De Cat, Cécile. 2005. "French Subject Clitics Are Not Agreement Markers." *Lingua* 115.9: 1195–219. doi:10.1016/j.lingua.2004.02.002.

Denson, David, and Richard Hogg. 2006. "Overview." In *A History of the English Language*. edited by Richard Hogg and David Denison, 1–42. Cambridge: Cambridge University Press.

Deshaies, Denise, and Ève Laforge. 1981. "Le futur simple et le futur proche dans le français parlé dans la ville de Québec." *Langues et linguistique* 7: 21–37. http://www.lli.ulaval.ca/fileadmin/llt/fichiers/recherche/revue_LL/vol07/LL7_21_37.pdf.

*Dictionary of Lousiana French: As Spoken in Cajun, Creole, and American Indian Communities*. 2010. Senior editor, Albert Valdman. Jackson: University of Mississippi Press.

Dion, Nathalie. 2003. "L'effacement du que en français canadien: Une étude en temps réel." M.A. thesis, University of Ottawa.

Ditchy, Jay K., ed. 1932. *Les acadiens louisianais et leur parler*. Paris: Droz.

Dubois, Lise, and Annette Boudreau, eds. 1996. *Les Acadiens et leur(s) langue(s): Quand le français est minoritaire; Actes du Colloque*. Moncton, N.B.: Éditions d'Acadie.

Dubois, Sylvie. 1995. "Field Method in Four Cajun Communities in Louisiana." In *French and Creole in Louisiana*, edited by Albert Valdman, 47–69. New York: Plenum.

Dubois, Sylvie, and Barbara Horvath. 1999. "When the Music Changes, You Change, Too: Gender and Language Change in Cajun English." *Language Variation and Change* 11.3: 287–313. doi:10.1017/S0954394599113036.

Dubois, Sylvie, Ruth King, and Terry Nadasdi. 2004. "Past and Present Agreements: A Comparison of Third Person Plural Marking in Acadian and Cajun French." Paper presented at Sociolinguistic Symposium 15, Newcastle, U.K., Aug. 1–4.

Dubois, Sylvie, and David Sankoff. 1996. "L'absence d'inflection sur les emprunts à l'anglais dans le français cadjin." Paper presented at the annual meeting of the Association francophone pour le savoir (Acfas), Montreal, May 13–17.

Dugas, Marie Alice. 1935. "A Glossary of the Variants from Standard-French Used in the Parish of St. James." M.A. thesis, Louisiana State University.

Emonds, Joseph E. 1976. *A Transformational Approach to English Syntax: Root, Structure-Preserving, and Local Transformations*. New York: Academic Press.

Elsig, Martin. 2009. *Grammatical Variation across Space and Time: The French Interrogative System*. Amsterdam: Benjamins.

Embick, David, and Rolf Noyer. 2007. "Distributed Morphology and the Syntax-Morphology Interface." In *The Oxford Handbook of Linguistic Interfaces*, edited by Gillian Ramchand and Charles Reiss, 289–324. Oxford: Oxford University Press.

Emirkanian, Louisette, and David Sankoff. 1985. "Le futur simple et le futur périphrastique dans le français parlé." In *Les tendances dynamiques du français parlé à Montréal*, edited by Monique Lemieux and Henrietta J. Cedergren, 189–204. Quebec: Office de la langue française, Gouvenement du Québec.

Emonds, Joseph. 1976. *A Transformational Approach to English Syntax*. New York: Academic Press.

Ernst, Gerhard. 1985. *Gesprochenes Französisch zu Beginn des 17. Jahrhunderts: Direkte Rede in Jean Héroards "Histoire particulière de Louis XIII" (1605–1610)*. Beihefte zur Zeitschrift für romanische Philologie 204. Tübingen: Niemeyer.

Esch, Edith. 2002. "My Dad's Auxiliaries." In *Language Change: The Interplay of Internal, External, and Extra-Linguistic Factors*, edited by Mari C. Jones and Edith Esch, 111–39. Berlin: Mouton de Gruyter.

Estienne, Henri. 1578. *Deux dialogues du nouveau langage francois*. Edited by Pauline M. Smith. Geneva: Slatkine, 1980.

Falkert, Anika. 2005. "Quelques spécificités du français acadien des Îles-de-la-Madeleine." In Brasseur and Falkert, 71–82.

Flikeid, Karin. 1989a. "'Moitié anglais, moitié français'? Emprunts et alternance de langues dans les communautés acadiennes de la Nouvelle-Écosse." *Revue québécoise de linguistique théorique et appliquée* 8.2: 177–227.

———. 1989b. "Recherches sociolinguistiques sur les parlers acadiens du Nouveau-Brunswick et de la Nouvelle-Écosse." In Mougeon and Beniak 1989, 183–200.

———. 1994. "Origines et évolution du français acadien à la lumière de l'étude de la diversité contemporaine." In Mougeon and Beniak 1994, 275–336.

Flikeid, Karin, and Louise Péronnet. 1989. "N'est-ce pas vrai qu'il faut dire 'J'avons été'? Divergences régionales en acadien." *Français moderne* 57.3/4: 219–28.

Fortier, Alcée. 1891. *The Acadians of Louisiana and Their Dialect*. Baltimore, Md.: Fortier.

———. 1894. *Louisiana Studies: Literature, Customs and Dialects, History and Education*. New Orleans, La.: Hansell.

Foulet, Lucien. 1921. "Comment ont évolué les formes de l'interrogation." *Romania: Recueil trimestriel des langues et des littératures romanes* 47: 243–348.

Fournier, Nathalie. 1998. *Grammaire du français classique*. Paris: Belin.

Fox, Cynthia A., and Jane S. Smith. 2005. "La situation du français franco-américain: Aspects linguistiques et sociolinguistiques." In Valdman, Auger, and Piston-Hatlen 2005, 117–44.

Frei, Henri. 1929. *La grammaire des fautes*. Paris-Genève ed. Geneva: Slatkine Reprints, 1971.

Gachignard, Pierre. 1983. *Dictionnaire du patois du marais poitevin: Particulièrement celui du canton de Maillezais et des communes voisines de Vendée, Charente-Maritime et Deux-Sèvres*. Marseille: Éditions Jeanne Lafitte.

Garner, John E. 1952. "A Descriptive Study of the Phonology of Acadian French." Ph.D. diss., University of Texas at Austin.

Geddes, James, Jr. 1893–94. "Comparison of Two Acadian French Dialects Spoken on the North-East of North America with the Franco-Canadian Dialect Spoken in Ste. Anne de Beaupré, Province of Quebec." *Modern Language Notes* 8.8: 225–30, doi:10.2307/2919367; 9.1: 1–6, doi:10.2307/2918766; 9.2: 50–58, doi:10.2307/2918731.

———. 1908. *Study of an Acadian-French Dialect Spoken on the North Shore of the Baie-des-Chaleurs.* Halle, Germany: Niemeyer.

Gérin, Pierre, and Pierre M. Gérin, eds. 1982. *Marichette: Lettres acadiennes, 1895–1898.* Sherbrooke, Que.: Éditions Naaman.

Gesner, B. Edward. 1979a. *Étude morphosyntaxique du parler acadien de la Baie Sainte-Marie, Nouvelle-Écosse (Canada).* Quebec: Centre international de recherche sur le bilinguisme.

———. 1979b. "L'emploi des auxiliaires *avoir* et *être* dans le parler de la Baie Sainte-Marie, Nouvelle-Écosse." In *Papers from the Second Annual Meeting of the Atlantic Provinces Linguistic Association, December 1–2, 1978, Halifax, Nova Scotia,* edited by George W. Patterson, 16–22. Halifax: Mount Saint Vincent University.

———. 1986. *Bibliographie annotée de linguistique acadienne.* Quebec: Centre internationale de recherches sur le bilinguisme.

Giancarli, Pierre-Don. 2011. *Les auxiliaires être et avoir: Étude comparée corse, français, acadien et anglais.* Rennes, France: Presses Universitaires de Rennes.

Gilliéron, J., and E. Édmont. 1902–10. *Atlas linguistique de la France.* Paris: Honoré Champion.

Goosse, André. 2000. "Évolution de la syntaxe." In *Histoire de la langue française, 1945–2000,* edited by Gérald Antoine and Bernard Cerquiglini, 107–45. Paris: CNRS.

Grevisse, Maurice. 1969. *Le bon usage: Grammaire française avec des remarques sur la langue française d'aujourd'hui.* 9th ed. Gembloux: Duculot.

———. 1986. *Le bon usage: Grammaire française.* Edited by André Goosse. 12th ed. Paris: Duculot.

Griffiths, Naomi E. S. 1992. *The Contexts of Acadian History, 1686–1784.* Montreal: McGill-Queen's University Press.

Grimm, Rick, and Terry Nadasdi. 2011. "The Future of Ontario French." *Journal of French Language Studies* 21.2: 173–90. doi:10.1017/S0959269510000335.

Guilbeau, John. 1936. "A Glossary of Variants from Standard French in Lafourche Parish." M.A. thesis, Louisiana State University.

———. 1952. "The French Spoken in Lafourche Parish." Ph.D. diss., University of North Carolina at Chapel Hill.

Guillaume, Gustave. 1929. *Temps et verbe: Théorie des aspects, des modes, et des temps.* Paris: Champion.

Haden, Ernest F. 1948. "La petite Cendrillouse, version acadienne de Cendrillon." *Archives de folklore* 3: 21–34.

Halle, Morris, and Alec Marantz. 1993. "Distributed Morphology and the Pieces of Inflection." In *The View from Building 20: Essays in Linguistics in Honor of Sylvain Bromberger,* edited by Kenneth Hale and Samuel Jay Keyser, 111–76. Cambridge, Mass.: MIT Press.

Harris, Alice C., and Lyle Campbell. 1995. *Historical Syntax in Cross-Linguistic Perspective*. Cambridge: Cambridge University Press.

Harris, Martin. 1978. *The Evolution of French Syntax: A Comparative Approach*. London: Longman.

Hatcher, Anna Granville. 1942. *Reflexive Verbs: Latin, Old French, Modern French*. Baltimore, Md.: Johns Hopkins Press.

Henry, Alison. 2002. "Variation and Syntactic Theory." In *The Handbook of Language Variation and Change*, edited by J. K. Chambers, Peter Trudgill, and Natalie Schilling-Estes, 267–82. Malden, Mass.: Blackwell.

Hickman, Frances Marion. 1940. "The French Speech of Jefferson Parish." M.A. thesis, Louisiana State University.

Hubert, Paul. 1938. "La langue française aux Îles-Madeleine." In *Deuxième congrès de la langue française au Canada, Québec, 27 juin–1 juillet 1937: Mémoires.*, vol. 1, 54–75. Quebec: Imprimerie de l'Action sociale.

Huddleston, Rodney, and Geoffrey K. Pullum 2002. *The Cambridge Grammar of the English Language*. Cambridge: Cambridge University Press.

Huot, Hélène. 1992. *La grammaire française entre comparatisme et structuralisme, 1870–1960*. Paris: A. Colin.

Jaubert, M. le comte [Hippolyte-François]. 1864. *Glossaire du centre de la France*. 2nd ed. Paris: Imprimerie et librairie centrales de Napoléon Chaix et Cie.

Jespersen, Otto. 1917. *Negation in English and Other Languages*. Copenhagen: Høst.

Johnstone, Barbara. 2011. "Dialect Enregisterment in Performance." *Journal of Sociolinguistics* 15.5: 657–79. doi:10.1111/j.1467-9841.2011.00512.x.

Jones, Mari C. 2001. *Jersey Norman French: A Lingusitic Study of an Obsolescent Dialect*. Oxford: Blackwell.

Jones, Michael Allan. 1996. *Foundations of French Syntax*. Cambridge: Cambridge University Press.

Kayne, Richard S. 1974. "French Relative *Que*." In *Current Studies in Romance Linguistics*, edited by Marta Luján and Fritz Hensey, 255–99. Washington, D.C.: Georgetown University Press.

Keenan, Edward L. 2002. "Explaining the Creation of Reflexive Pronouns in English." In *Studies in the History of the English Language: A Millennial Perspective*, edited by Donka Minkova and Robert Stockwell, 325–54. Berlin: Mouton de Gruyter.

King, Ruth. 1978. "Étude phonologique et morphologique du parler français de l'Anse-à-Canards (Baie St-Georges, Terre-Neuve), suivie d'un lexique." M.A. thesis, Memorial University of Newfoundland.

———. 1983. "Variation and Change in Newfoundland French: A Sociolinguistic Study of Clitic Pronouns." Ph.D. diss., Memorial University of Newfoundland.

———. 1989. "Le français terreneuvien: Aperçu général." In Mougeon and Beniak 1989, 227–44.

———. 1991. "WH-words, WH-questions, and Relative Clauses in Prince Edward Island French." *Canadian Journal of Linguistics* 36.1: 65–85.

———. 1994. "Subject-Verb Agreement in Newfoundland French." *Language Variation and Change* 6.3: 239–53. doi:10.1017/S0954394500001678.

———. 2000. *The Lexical Basis of Grammatical Borrowing: A Prince Edward Island French Case Study*. Amsterdam: Benjamins.

———. 2005a. "Crossing Grammatical Borders: Tracing the Path of Contact-Induced Linguistic Change." In *Dialects across Borders: Selected Papers from the 11th International Conference on Methods in Dialectology (Methods XI), Joensuu, August 2002*, edited by Markku Filppula, Juhani Klemola, Marjatta Palander, and Esa Penttilä, 233–51. Amsterdam: Benjamins.

———. 2005b. "Morphosyntactic Variation and Theory: Subject-Verb Agreement in Acadian French." In Cornips and Corrigan, 199–229.

———. 2008. "*Chiac* in Context: Overview and Evaluation of Acadie's *Joual*." In *Social Lives in Language: Sociolinguistics and Multilingual Speech Communities*, edited by Miriam Meyerhoff and Naomi Nagy, 137–78. Amsterdam: Benjamins.

———. 2011. "Back to *Back*: The Trajectory of an Old Borrowing." In *Le français en contact: Hommages à Raymond Mougeon*, edited by France Martineau and Terry Nadasdi, 193–216. Quebec: Presses de l'Université Laval.

———. 2013. "Morphosyntactic Variation." In *The Oxford Handbook of Sociolinguistics*, edited by Robert Bayley, Richard Cameron, and Ceil Lucas. Oxford: Oxford University Press.

King, Ruth, and Gary Butler. 2005. "Les Franco-Terreneuviens et le franco-terre-neuvien." In Valdman, Auger, and Piston-Hatlen 2005, 169–86.

King, Ruth, France Martineau, and Raymond Mougeon. 2011. "The Interplay of Internal and External Factors in Grammatical Change: First-Person Plural Pronouns in French." *Language* 87.3: 470–509. doi:10.1353/lan.2011.0072.

King, Ruth, and Terry Nadasdi. 1996. "Sorting Out Morphosyntactic Variation in Acadian French: The Importance of the Linguistic Marketplace." In *Sociolinguistic Variation: Data, Theory, and Analysis; Selected Papers from NWAV 23 at Stanford*, edited by Jennifer Arnold, Renee Blake, Brad Davidson, Scott Schwenter, and Julie Solomon, 113–28. Stanford, Calif.: Center for the Study of Language and Information.

———. 1997. "Left Dislocation, Number Marking, and (Non-)Standard French." *Probus* 9.3: 267–84. doi:10.1515/prbs.1997.9.3.267.

———. 1999. "The Expression of Evidentiality in French-English Bilingual Discourse." *Language in Society* 28.3: 355–66. doi:10.1017/S0047404599003024.

———. 2003. "Back to the Future in Acadian French." *Journal of French Language Studies* 13.3: 323–37. doi:10.1017/S0959269503001157.

———. 2005. "Deux auxiliaires qui voulaient *mourir* en français acadien." In Brasseur and Falkert, 103–12.

———. 2006. "Another Look at Que-Deletion." Paper presented at the 35th annual meeting on New Ways of Analysis of Variation (NWAV 35), Columbus, Ohio, Nov. 9–12.

———. 2013. "Morphosyntactic Variation." In *The Oxford Handbook of Sociolinguistics*, edited by Robert Bayley, Richard Cameron, and Ceil Lucas, 445–63. Oxford: Oxford University Press.

King, Ruth, Terry Nadasdi, and Gary R. Butler. 2004. "First Person Plural in Prince Edward Island Acadian French: The Fate of the Vernacular Variant *je … ons.*" *Language Variation and Change* 16.3: 237–55. doi:10.1017/S0954394504163035.

King, Ruth, and Yves Roberge. 1990. "Preposition Stranding in Prince Edward Island French." *Probus* 2.3: 351–69. doi:10.1515/prbs.1990.2.3.351.

King, Ruth, and Robert W. Ryan. 1991. "Dialect Contact vs. Dialect Isolation: Nasal Vowels in Atlantic Canada Acadian French." In *Proceedings of the Fourteenth International Congress of Linguists: Berlin/GDR, August 10–August 15, 1987*, edited by Werner Bahner, Joachim Schildt, and Dieter Viehweger, 1512–15. Berlin: Akademie-Verlag.

Kiss, Katalin É. 1998. "Identificational Focus versus Information Focus." *Language* 74.2: 245–73. doi:10.2307/417867.

Labelle, Ronald. 2001. "Les contes folkloriques acadiens." *Bulletin ICOM Canada, Conseil international des musées* 13. http://www.umoncton.ca/crmea/files/crmea/wf/wf/Les_contes_folkloriques_acadiens.pdf.

Labov, William. 1982. "Speech Actions and Reactions in Personal Narrative." In *Analyzing Discourse: Text and Talk*, edited by Deborah Tannen, 219–47 Washington, D.C.: Georgetown University Press.

———. 1997. "Some Further Steps in Narrative Analysis." In "Oral Versions of Personal Experience: Three Decades of Narrative Analysis," edited by Michael G. W. Bamberg. Special issue, *Journal of Narrative and Life History* 7.1–4: 395–415.

Labov, William, and Joshua Waletzky. 1967. "Narrative Analysis: Oral Versions of Personal Experience." In *Essays on the Verbal and Visual Arts*, edited by June Helm, 12–44. Seattle: University of Washington Press.

Lavandera, Beatriz R. 1978. "Where Does the Sociolinguistic Variable Stop?" *Language in Society* 7.2: 171–82. doi:10.1017/S0047404500005510.

Law, Paul. 1998. "A Unified Account of P-stranding in Romance and Germanic." In *Proceedings of the North East Linguistic Society 28: University of Toronto*, edited by Pius N. Tamanji and Kiyomi Kusumoto, 219–34. Amherst, Mass.: Graduate Linguistic Student Association.

———. 2006. "Preposition Stranding." In *The Blackwell Companion to Syntax*, edited by Martin Everaert and Henk van Riemsdijk, 3: 631–84. Oxford: Blackwell. doi:10.1002/9780470996591.ch51.

LeBlanc, Carmen. 2011. "Le français madelinot: Transmission de la langue et changements générationnels." Paper presented at Methods in Dialectology 14, London, Ont., Aug. 2–6.

LeBlanc, Dano. 2007. *Acadieman comics: Ses origines.* Moncton, N.B.: Les Éditions Court Circuit.

———. 2009. *Les aventures Acadieman #3: Ses origines: Les strips 2002–2009.* Memramcook, N.B.: Productions Mudworld.

Ledgeway, Adam. 2000. *A Comparative Syntax of the Dialects of Southern Italy: A Minimalist Approach.* Oxford: Blackwell.

————. 2011. "Syntactic and Morphosyntactic Typology and Change." In *The Cambridge History of the Romance Languages*, vol. 1, edited by Martin Maiden, John Charles Smith, and Adam Ledgeway, 382–471. Cambridge: Cambridge University Press.

Legendre, Napoléon. 1890. *La langue française au Canada*. Quebec: Darveau.

Lemieux, Monique, Marielle Saint-Amour, and David Sankoff. 1985. "/TUT/ en français de Montréal: Un cas de neutralisation morphologique." In *Les tendances dynamiques du français parlé à Montréal*, vol. 2, edited by Monique Lemieux and Henrietta J. Cedergren, 7–91. Quebec: Gouvernement du Québec.

Leroux, Martine. 2005. "Past, but Not Gone: The Past Temporal Reference System in Quebec French." In "Papers from NWAV33," edited by Suzanne Evans Wagner. *University of Pennsylvania Working Papers in Linguistics* 11.2: 119–31.

Lightfoot, David. 2006. *How New Languages Emerge*. Cambridge: Cambridge University Press.

Lipski, John M. 1990. *The Language of the Isleños: Vestigial Spanish in Louisiana*. Baton Rouge: Louisiana State University Press.

Littré, Émile. 1968. *Dictionnaire de la langue française*. Vol. 2. Paris: Gallimard, Hachette.

Lodge, R. Anthony. 2004. *A Sociolinguistic History of Parisian French*. Cambridge: Cambridge University Press.

Long, Michael. 2008. "Les verbes à particule (VPART) dans une variété de français acadien, le chiac." M.A. thesis, Université de Moncton.

Longobardi, Giuseppe. 2001. "Formal Syntax, Diachronic Minimalism, and Etymology: The History of French *chez*." *Linguistic Inquiry* 32.2: 275–302. doi: 10.1162/00243890152001771.

Lucci, Vincent. 1972. *Phonologie de l'acadien: Parler de la région de Moncton, N.B., Canada*. Montreal: Didier.

Macaulay, Ronald. 2006. "Pure Grammaticalization: The Development of a Teenage Intensifer." *Language Variation and Change* 18.3: 267–83. doi:10.1017/S095 4394506060133.

Magord, André, Rodrigue Landry, and Réal Allard. 2002. "La vitalité ethnolinguistique de la communauté franco-terreneuvienne de la peninsula de Port-au-Port: Une étude comparative." In *Les Franco-Terreneuviens de la péninsule de Port-au-Port: Évolution d'une identité franco-canadienne*, edited by André Magord, 197–228. Moncton, N.B.: Chaire d'études acadiennes, Université de Moncton.

Martineau, France. 1988. "Variable Deletion of *que* in the Spoken French of Ottawa-Hull." In *Advances in Romance Linguistics*, edited by David Birdsong and Jean-Pierre Montreuil, 275–87. Dordrect: Foris.

————. 1993. "Rection forte et rection faible des verbes: L'ellipse de *que* en français du Québec et de l'Ontario." *Francophonies d'Amérique* 3: 79–90.

————. 2005. "Perspectives sur le changement linguistique: Aux sources du français canadien." *Canadian Journal of Linguistics* 50: 173–213. doi:10.1353/cjl .2007.0010.

Martineau, France, and Raymond Mougeon. 2003. "A Sociolinguistic Study of the Origins of *ne* Deletion in European and Quebec French." *Language* 79.1: 118–52. doi:10.1353/lan.2003.0090.

Martineau, France, and Sandrine Tailleur. 2011. "Written Vernacular: Variation and Change in 19th Century Acadian French." In *On Linguistic Change in French: Socio-Historical Approaches; Studies in Honour of Professor R. Anthony Lodge*, edited by Tim Pooley and Dominique Lagorgette, 153–74. Chambéry: Université de Savoie.

Martinet, André. 1955. *Économie des changements phonétiques: Traité de phonologie diachronique*. Berne: Francke.

———. 1979. *Grammaire fonctionnelle du français*. Paris: Didier.

Massignon, Geneviève. 1947. "Les parlers français d'Acadie." *French Review* 21.1: 45–53.

———. 1962. *Les parlers français d'Acadie: Enquête linguistique*. 2 vols. Paris: Klincksieck.

Maurais, Jacques. 1993. "État de la recherce sur la description de la francophonie au Québec." In *Le français dans l'espace francophone: Description linguistique et sociolinguistique de la francophonie*, vol. 1, edited by Didier de Robillard and Michel Beniamino, 79–98. Paris: Champion.

McKillop, Anne. 1987. "Une étude sociolinguistique du parler 'brayon' d'Edmunston au Nouveau-Brunswick." M.A. thesis, University of New Brunswick.

Meechan, Marjory, and Shana Poplack. 1995. "Orphan Categories in Bilingual Discourse: Adjectivization Strategies in Wolof-French and Fongbe-French." *Language Variation and Change* 7.2: 169–94. doi:10.1017/S0954394500000971.

Ménétra, Jacques-Louis. 1998. *Journal de ma vie: Compagnon vitrier au XVIIIe siècle*. Paris: Albin Michel.

Milroy, James, and Lesley Milroy. 1987. *Authority in Language: Investigating Language Prescription and Standardisation*. London: Routledge & Kegan Paul.

Milroy, Lesley. 1980. *Language and Social Networks*. Oxford: Blackwell.

Montgomery, Erin. 1946. "A Glossary of Variants from Standard French in Vermillion Parish." M.A. thesis, Louisiana State University.

Morin, Yves-Charles. 1985. "On the Two French Subjectless Verbs *voici* and *violà*." *Language* 61.4: 777–820. doi:10.2307/414490.

Mougeon, Raymond, and Édouard Beniak, eds. 1989. *Le français canadien parlé hors Québec: Aperçu sociolinguistique*. Quebec: Presses de l'Université Laval.

———. 1991. *Linguistic Consequences of Language Contact and Restriction: The Case of French in Ontario, Canada*. Oxford: Clarendon.

———, eds. 1994. *Les origines du français québécois*. Sainte-Foy, Quebec: Presses de l'Université Laval.

Mougeon, Raymond, and Pierre Hébrard. 1975. "Aspects de l'assimilation linguistique dans une communauté francophone de l'Ontario." *Working Papers on Bilingualism* 5: 1–38. Bilingual Education Project, Ontario Institute for Studies in Education, Toronto.

Nadasdi, Terry. 2000. *Variation grammaticale et langue minoritaire: Le cas des pronoms clitiques en français ontarian.* Munich: LINCOM Europa.

Nyrop, Kristoffer. 1899–1930. *Grammaire historique de la langue française.* 4th ed. 6 vols. Copenhagen: Bojesen.

*OED Online. Oxford English Dictionary.* Oxford University Press. http://www.oed.com/.

Peacock, Kenneth. 1965. *Songs of the Newfoundland Outports.* 3 vols. Ottawa: National Museum of Canada.

Pelmont, André Prosper. 1994. *Glossaire du patois d'Hérisson: Commune de Pougne-Hérisson, arrondissement de Parthenay, Deux-Sèvres.* Prahecq, France: Geste éditions.

Péronnet, Louise. 1975. "Modalités nominales et verbales dans le parler franco-acadien de la région du sud-est du Nouveau-Brunswick." M.A. thesis, Université de Moncton.

———. 1989. *Le parler acadien du Sud-Est du Nouveau-Brunswick: Éléments grammaticaux et lexicaux.* New York: Peter Lang.

———. 1991. "Système de modalités verbales dans le parler acadien du sud-est du Nouveau-Brunswick." *Journal of the Atlantic Provinces Linguistic Association* 13: 85–98.

———. 1995. "L'apport de la tradition orale à la description linguistique." *Francophonies d'Amérique* 5: 37–44. doi:10.7202/1004524ar.

Péronnet, Louise, Rose Mary Babitch, Wladyslaw Cichocki, and Patrice Brasseur. 1998. *Atlas linguistique du vocabulaire maritime acadien.* Sainte-Foy, Quebec: Presses de l'Université Laval.

Perrot, Marie-Éve. 1995. "Aspects fondamentaux du métissage français/anglais dans le chiac du Moncton (Nouveau-Brunswick, Canada)." Ph.D. diss., Université de la Sorbonne.

Pesetsky, David, and Esther Torrego. 2001. "T-to-C Movement: Causes and Consequences." In *Ken Hale: A Life in Language,* edited by Michael Kenstowicz, 355–426. Cambridge, Mass.: MIT Press.

Petraş, Christina. 2005. "Valeurs pragmatiques du contact de langues au niveau des marqueurs discursifs dans un corpus acadien." In *Français d'Amérique: Approches morphosyntaxiques; Actes du colloque international Grammaire comparée des variétés de français d'Amérique,* edited by Patrice Brasseur and Anika Falkert, 275–88. Paris: L'Harmattan.

Picone, Michael D. 1993. "Lexical Code-Switching in Louisiana French." Paper presented at the 22nd annual meeting on New Ways of Analyzing Variation in English (NWAVE 22), Ottawa, Oct. 14–17.

Poirier, Pascal. 1884. "La langue acadienne." *Nouvelles soirées canadiennes* 3: 63–70.

Poplack, Shana. 1992. "The Inherent Variability of the French Subjunctive." In *Theoretical Analyses in Romance Linguistics: Selected Papers from the Nineteenth Linguistic Symposium on Romance Languages (LSRL XIX), The Ohio State University, 21–23 April 1989,* edited by Christiane Laeufer and Terrell A. Morgan, 235–63. Amsterdam: Benjamins.

————, ed. 2000. *The English History of African American English.* Malden, Mass.: Blackwell.

Poplack, Shana, and Nathalie Dion. 2009. "Prescription vs. Praxis: The Evolution of Future Temporal Reference in French." *Language* 85.3: 557–87. doi:10.1353/lan.0.0149.

Poplack, Shana, and Danielle Turpin. 1999. "Does the *futur* Have a Future in (Canadian) French?" *Probus* 11.1: 133–64. doi:10.1515/prbs.1999.11.1.133.

Reinhart, Tanya, and Tal Siloni. 2005. "The Lexicon-Syntax Parameter: Reflexivization and Other Arity Operations." *Linguistic Inquiry* 36.3: 389–436. doi:10.1162/0024389054396881.

Rézeau, Pierre. 1976. *Un patois de Vendée: Le parler rural du Vouvant.* Paris: Klincksieck.

Rickford, John R. 1998. "The Creole Origins of African-American Vernacular English: Evidence from Copula Absence." In *African-American English: Structure, History, and Use,* edited by Salikoko S. Mufwene, John R. Rickford, Guy Bailey, and John Baugh, 154–200. London: Routledge.

————. 2006. "Down for the Count? The Creole Origins Hypothesis of AAVE at the Hands of the Ottawa Circle, and Their Supporters." Review of Poplack 2000. *Journal of Pidgin and Creole Languages* 21.1: 97–155. doi:10.1075/jpcl.21.1.03ric.

Rideout, Douglas L. 2011. "Auxiliary Selection in 16th Century French: Imposing Norms in the Face of Language Change." In "Selected Proceedings of the 33rd Atlantic Provinces Linguistics Association," edited by Sara Johanson, Evan Hazenberg, and Suzanne Power. *Memorial University of Newfoundland Occasional Papers in Linguistics* 2. http://www.mun.ca/linguistics/MLWP/Rideout_2011.pdf.

Rizzi, Luigi. 1989. Preface of *La variation dialectale en grammaire universelle,* by Yves Roberge and Marie-Thérèse Vinet, 8–10. Montreal: Presses de l'Université de Montréal.

————. 1990. *Relativized Minimality.* Cambridge, Mass.: MIT Press.

Roberge, Yves. 1990. *The Syntactic Recoverability of Null Arguments.* Kingston, Ont.: McGill-Queen's University Press.

Roberge, Yves, and Nicole Rosen. 1999. "Preposition Stranding and *que*-Deletion in Varieties of North American French." *Linguistics Atlantica* 21: 153–68.

Robert, Paul. 1985. *Le Grand Robert de la langue française: Dictionnaire alphabétique et analogique de la langue française.* Edited by Alain Rey. 2nd ed. Paris: Le Robert.

Roberts, Ian G. 1993. *Verbs and Diachronic Syntax: A Comparative History of English and French.* Dordrecht: Kluwer.

————. 2007. *Diachronic Syntax.* Oxford University Press.

Roberts, Nicholas. 2011. "*Le futur commence après la fin de cette phrase*: The Future of French Future." Paper presented at the 40th annual meeting on New Ways of Analyzing Variation (NWAV40), Washington D.C., Oct. 27–30.

Ross, Sally, and Alphonse Deveau. 1992. *The Acadians of Nova Scotia: Past and Present.* Halifax, N.S.: Nimbus.

Rottet, Kevin J. 2000. "The Calquing of Phrasal Verbs in Language Contact." In "The CVC of Sociolinguistics: Contact, Variation, and Culture," edited by Julie

Auger and Andrea Word-Allbritton. *Indiana University Working Papers in Linguistics* 2: 109–26.

———. 2001. *Language Shift in the Coastal Marshes of Louisiana.* New York: Lang.

———. 2005. "Phrasal Verbs and English Influence on Welsh." *Word* 56.1: 39–70.

Rowlett, Paul. 2007. *The Syntax of French.* Cambridge: Cambridge University Press.

Roy, Marie-Marthe. 1979. "Les conjonctions anglaises *but* et *so* dans le français de Moncton: Une étude sociolinguistique de changements linguistiques provoqués par une situation de contact." M.A. thesis, Université du Québec à Montréal.

Russo, Marijke, and Julie Roberts. 1999. "Linguistic Change in Endangered Dialects: The Case of Alternation between *avoir* and *être* in Vermont French." *Language Variation and Change* 11.1: 67–86. doi:10.1017/S0954394599111049.

Ryan, Robert W. 1981. *Analyse morphologique du groupe verbal du parler franco-acadien de la région de la Baie Sainte-Marie, Nouvelle-Écosse (Canada).* Quebec: Centre international de recherche sur le bilinguisme.

Sankoff, David, and Suzanne Laberge. 1978. "The Linguistic Market and the Statistical Explanation of Variability." In *Linguistic Variation: Models and Methods,* edited by David Sankoff, 239–50. New York: Academic Press.

Sankoff, David, Sali A. Tagliamonte, and Eric Smith. 2012. Goldvarb Lion: A Multivariate Analysis Application. http://individual.utoronto.ca/tagliamonte/goldvarb.htm.

Sankoff, Gillian. 1980. *The Social Life of Language.* Philadelphia: University of Pennsylvania Press.

Sankoff, Gillian, and Pierrette Thibault. 1980. "The Alternation between the Auxiliaries *avoir* and *être* in Montreal French." In *The Social Life of Language,* edited by Gillian Sankoff, 311–46. Philadelphia: University of Pennsylvania Press. Translation of "L'alternance entre les auxiliaires *avoir* et *être* dans le français parlé à Montréal." *Langue française* 34 (1977): 81–108.

Sankoff, Gillian, Pierrette Thibault, and Suzanne Evans Wagner. 2004. "An Apparent Time Paradox: Change in Montréal French Auxiliary Selection, 1971–1995." Paper presented at 33rd annual meeting on New Ways of Analyzing Variation (NWAV 33), Ann Arbor, Mich., Sept. 30–Oct. 3.

Saucier, Corinne L. 1956. *Traditions de la paroisse des Avoyelles en Louisiane.* Philadelphia: American Folklore Society.

Seutin, Émile. 1975. *Description grammaticale du parler de l'Île-aux-Coudres, Québec.* Montreal: Presses de l'Université de Montréal.

Silva-Corvalán, Carmen. 1994. *Language Contact and Change: Spanish in Los Angeles.* Oxford: Clarendon.

Sorace, Antonella. 2000. "Gradients in Auxiliary Selection with Intransitive Verbs." *Language* 76.4: 859–90. doi:10.2307/417202.

Stäbler, Cynthia K. 1995. *La vie dans le temps et asteur: Ein Korpus von Gesprächen mit Cadiens in Louisiana.* Tübingen: Narr.

Statistics Canada. 2006. *Canadian Census of 2006.* Ottawa: Ministry of Supplies and Services.

Stoffel, Cornelis. 1901. *Intensives and Down-Toners: A Study in English Adverbs*. Heidelberg: Carl Winter's Universitätsbuchhandlung.

Stowell, Timothy. 1981. "Origins of Phrase Structure." Ph.D. diss., Massachussetts Institute of Technology.

———. 1982. "Conditions on Reanalysis." In "Papers in Syntax," edited by Alec Marantz and Tim Stowell. *MIT Working Papers in Linguistics* 4: 245–69.

Suñer, Margarita. 1994. "V-Movement and the Licensing of Argumental WH-Phrases in Spanish." *Natural Language and Linguistic Theory* 12.2: 335–72. doi: 10.1007/BF00993148.

Svenson, Lars Owe. 1959. *Les parlers du Marais Vendéen*. Vol. 1, *Phonétique, morphologie et syntaxe, textes, onamastique, lexique*. Göteborg: Elander.

Tagliamonte, Sali. 2002. "Comparative Sociolinguistics." In *The Handbook of Language Variation and Change*, edited by J. K. Chambers, Peter Trudgill, and Natalie Schilling-Estes, 729–63. Malden, Mass.: Blackwell.

Tagliamonte, Sali, and Chris Roberts. 2005. "So Weird; So Cool; So Innovative: The Use of Intensifiers in the Television Series *Friends*." *American Speech* 80.3: 280–300. doi:10.1215/00031283-80-3-280.

Tailleur, Sandrine. 2007. "L'alternance d'emploi des auxiliaires avoir et être avec les verbes intransitifs en français du XVIIIe siècle." M.A. thesis, Université d'Ottawa.

Thomas, Gerald. 1983. *Les deux traditions: Le conte populaire chez les Franco-Terreneuviens*. Montreal: Bellarmin.

Traugott, Elizabeth Closs. 2006. "The Semantic Development of Scalar Focus Modifiers." In *The Handbook of the History of English*, edited by Ans van Kemenade and Bettelou Los, 335–59. Oxford: Blackwell.

Tuller, Laurice Anne. 1986. "Bijective Relations in Universal Grammar and the Syntax of Hausa." Ph.D. diss., University of California, Los Angeles.

Turpin, Danielle. 1998. "'Le français, c'est le *last frontier*': The Status of English-Origin Nouns in Acadian French." *International Journal of Bilingualism* 2.2: 221–33. doi:10.1177/13670069800200206.

Valdman, Albert. 1979. *Le Français hors de France*. Paris: Champion.

Valdman, Albert, Julie Auger, and Deborah Piston-Hatlen, eds. 2005. *Le français en Amérique du Nord: État présent*. Quebec: Presses de l'Université Laval.

Vaugelas, Claude Favre de. 1690. *Nouvelles remarques sur la langue française, utiles à ceux qui veulent bien parler et bien écrire*. Paris: Louis-Augustin Allemand.

Vincent, Diane. 1984. "Le sacre au Québec: Transgression d'un ordre religieux ou social?" *Culture* 4.2: 55–61.

Vinet, Marie-Thérèse. 1984. "La syntaxe du québécois et les emprunts à l'anglais." *Revue de l'Association québécoise de linguistique* 3.3: 221–42.

———. 2001. *D'un français à l'autre: La syntaxe de la microvariation*. Saint-Laurent, Quebec: Fides.

Wagner, Robert Léon, and Jacqueline Pichon. 1991. *Grammaire du français: Classique et moderne*. Paris: Hachette.

Wagner, Suzanne Evans, and Gillian Sankoff. 2011. "Age Grading in the Montréal French Inflected Future." *Language Variation and Change* 23.3: 275–313. doi:10.1017/S0954394511000111.

Walker, Douglas. 2004. "Le vernaculaire en Alberta." In "Le français dans l'Ouest canadien (symposium du 31 mai 2004)," edited by Robert A. Papen and Dans A. Fauchon. Special issue, *Cahiers franco-canadiens de l'ouest* 16.1/2: 53–65.

Warren, Jane. 1994. "Plus ça change, plus c'est pareil: The case of 'que' in Montreal French." *Culture* 14.2: 39–49.

Wartburg, Walther von. 1966. *Französisches etymologisches Wörterbuch: Eine Darstellung des galloromanischen Sprachschatzes.* Basel: Zbinden.

Wheeler, Max W. 1988. "Catalan." In *The Romance Languages,* edited by Martin Harris and Nigel Vincent, 170–208. London: Routledge.

Wiesmath, Raphaëlle. 2000. "Enchaînement des propositions dans le Français acadien du Nouveau-Brunswick/Canada: Place de ce parler parmi d'autres variétés d'outre-mer." Ph.D. diss., Universität Freiburg.

Willis, Lauren A. 2000. "Être ou ne plus être: Auxiliary Alternation in Ottawa-Hull French." M.A. thesis, University of Ottawa.

Winford, Donald. 1997. "On the Origins of African American Vernacular English—A Creolist Perspective: Part 1: The Sociohistorical Background." *Diachronica* 14.2: 305–44. doi:10.1075/dia.14.2.05win.

———. 1998. "On the Origins of African American Vernacular English—A Creolist Perspective: Part 2: Linguistic Features." *Diachronica* 15.1: 99–154. doi: 10.1075/dia.15.1.05win.

Young, Hilary A. N. 2002. "'C'est either que tu parles français, c'est either que tu parles anglais': A Cognitive Approach to Chiac as a Contact Language." Ph.D. diss., Rice University.

Zink, Gaston. 1997. *Morphosyntaxe du pronom personnel (non réfléchi) en moyen français (XIVe–XVe siècles).* Geneva: Droz.

Zribi-Hertz, Anne. 1984. "Prépositions orphelines et pronoms nuls." *Recherches linguistiques de Vincennes* 12: 46–91.

Zubizarreta, Maria Luisa. 1998. *Prosody, Focus, and Word Order.* Cambridge, Mass.: MIT Press.

# INDEX

Page numbers in italics refer to figures and tables.